THE CHOSEN PEOPLE

Script by Iva Hoth
Illustrations by Andre Le Blanc
Bible editor, C. Elvan Olmstead, Ph.D.

Chariot Books
from
David C. Cook

A Giant's Challenge

ROM 1 SAMUEL 16: 23—17: 26

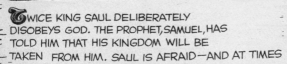

WICE KING SAUL DELIBERATELY DISOBEYS GOD. THE PROPHET, SAMUEL, HAS TOLD HIM THAT HIS KINGDOM WILL BE TAKEN FROM HIM. SAUL IS AFRAID—AND AT TIMES

HIS MIND BECOMES UNBALANCED. WHEN HIS ADVISORS TELL HIM ABOUT DAVID, A YOUNG SHEPHERD, WHO SINGS AND PLAYS A HARP, SAUL SENDS FOR HIM. DAVID ARRIVES AT THE PALACE...

THE KING IS VERY ILL TODAY—SO HE MAY BE DANGEROUS. NEVER TAKE YOUR EYES OFF HIM.

QUIETLY DAVID ENTERS THE KING'S ROOM AND BEGINS TO PLAY...SAUL STARES AT HIM WILDLY... BUT DAVID CONTINUES TO PLAY AND SING OF HIS FAITH IN GOD.

AT LAST KING SAUL RELAXES AND FALLS QUIETLY ASLEEP. AFTER THAT DAVID IS OFTEN CALLED TO THE PALACE. HIS MUSIC QUIETS SAUL'S TORTURED MIND—AND IN TIME THE KING SEEMS WELL AGAIN.

AND WHEN WORD COMES THAT THE PHILISTINES ARE PREPARING FOR AN ATTACK, SAUL LEADS HIS ARMY AGAINST THEM. DAVID'S THREE OLDEST BROTHERS JOIN THE KING'S FORCES.

ONE EVENING DAVID COMES IN FROM THE FIELDS TO FIND HIS FATHER BUSY PACKING FOOD.

THIS IS FOR YOUR BROTHERS. I WANT YOU TO TAKE IT TO THEM.

I'LL LEAVE RIGHT AWAY. WHAT'S THE LATEST NEWS FROM THE FRONT?

NOT GOOD, AND I'M WORRIED.

WHEN DAVID REACHES THE ISRAELITE CAMP, HE FINDS THE SOLDIERS STRANGELY QUIET.

WHAT'S THE MATTER?

SEND OUT A MAN WHO DARES TO FIGHT ME. IF HE KILLS ME, THE PHILISTINES WILL BE YOUR SERVANTS, BUT IF I KILL HIM, YOU WILL BE OUR SERVANTS.

...HE MATTER? ...STEN TO THAT GIANT!

WHO IS THAT PHILISTINE THAT HE CAN DEFY THE ARMY OF GOD?

THAT'S THE GIANT, GOLIATH—THE BIGGEST, STRONGEST, MOST FEARED OF ALL THE PHILISTINE SOLDIERS. NO MAN DARES TO TAKE UP HIS CHALLENGE.

NO MAN? IS EVERY ISRAELITE SOLDIER A COWARD?

THOSE ARE STRONG WORDS, BOY. BUT—LOOK—HERE COMES YOUR BIG BROTHER. YOU'D BETTER GET OUT OF HERE BEFORE HE HEARS WHAT YOU'VE SAID.

The Challenge Is Met

FROM 1 SAMUEL 17: 28-48

WHEN DAVID REACHES THE ISRAELITE CAMP, HE FINDS THAT NO ISRAELITE SOLDIER IS BRAVE ENOUGH TO ACCEPT THE PHILISTINE GIANT'S CHALLENGE TO FIGHT. DAVID IS ANGRY—BUT SO IS ELIAB, HIS BIG BROTHER...

WHAT ARE **YOU** DOING HERE? WHY AREN'T YOU HOME WHERE YOU BELONG —TAKING CARE OF THE SHEEP?

FATHER SENT ME HERE WITH FOOD FOR YOU—NOW **YOU** TELL ME WHY NO ONE HAS ACCEPTED GOLIATH'S CHALLENGE TO FIGHT?

EVER SINCE THE PROPHET SAMUEL CHOSE DAVID INSTEAD OF HIM, ELIAB HAS BEEN FILLED WITH JEALOUSY...NOW IT BURSTS INTO THE OPEN.

YOU'RE JUST A SHOW-OFF.

I'M NOT AFRAID. I'LL FIGHT THE GIANT.

MEANWHILE IN KING SAUL'S TENT.

EVERY DAY THAT GIANT DEFIES US I HAVE OFFERED A HANDSOME REWARD —EVEN MY DAUGHTER IN MARRIAGE— BUT NOT ONE SOLDIER IN MY WHOLE ARMY WILL ACCEPT THE CHALLENGE.

O KING— THERE IS ONE OUTSIDE WHO ACCEPTS, BUT—

BRING HIM HERE AT ONCE!

DAVID ENTERS—BUT SAUL DOES NOT REMEMBER THE SHEPHERD WHO PLAYED FOR HIM.

A SHEPHERD BOY! YOU CAN'T FIGHT A GIANT!

THE LORD WHO HELPED ME KILL A LION AND A BEAR WILL HELP ME NOW.

MAYBE YOU'RE RIGHT— AT LEAST YOU HAVE COURAGE. GO, AND THE LORD BE WITH THEE. YOU CAN WEAR MY OWN ARMOR.

I CAN'T WEAR THIS— I'M NOT USED TO FIGHTING IN ARMOR. BESIDES, MY PLAN IS NOT TO DEFEND MYSELF, BUT TO ATTACK!

WHEN THE ARMY RETURNS, SAUL'S GENERAL, ABNER, TAKES DAVID TO SEE THE KING.

YOU SAVED ISRAEL, DAVID. FROM NOW ON YOU WILL LIVE IN THE PALACE. PRINCE JONATHAN WILL TAKE YOU BACK WITH HIM.

DAVID AND JONATHAN BECOME TRUE FRIENDS— AND MAKE A PACT OF FRIENDSHIP.

DAVID, I'M PROUD TO BE THE FRIEND OF THE BRAVEST MAN IN ISRAEL. I WANT TO GIVE YOU MY ROBE AND ARMOR AS A SIGN THAT I WILL BE LOYAL TO YOU—FOREVER!

THANK YOU, JONATHAN. GOD IS MY WITNESS THAT I WILL BE YOUR FRIEND UNTIL DEATH.

TRIUMPHANTLY, KING SAUL AND HIS VICTORIOUS SOLDIERS RETURN HOME...THE WOMEN RUSH OUT OF THE CITIES TO GREET THEM AND SING THEIR PRAISES.

SAUL HAS SLAIN HIS THOUSANDS—AND DAVID HIS TEN THOUSANDS!

WHEN SAUL HEARS THESE WORDS, HE THINKS OF WHAT THE PROPHET SAMUEL TOLD HIM: "BECAUSE YOU HAVE DISOBEYED GOD, YOUR KINGDOM WILL BE GIVEN TO ANOTHER."

THE PEOPLE KNOW DAVID IS A GREATER WARRIOR THAN I. MAYBE _HE'S_ THE ONE WHO WILL TAKE MY KINGDOM FROM ME!

THAT NIGHT SAUL CANNOT SLEEP.

DAVID! HE'S THE HERO NOW! BUT HE CAN'T TAKE MY KINGDOM FROM ME—IF HE'S DEAD!

The Angry King

FROM 1 SAMUEL 19: 22—20: 33

THREE TIMES SAUL SENDS MEN TO RAMAH TO CAPTURE DAVID. BUT EACH TIME THE MEN FAIL. IN A FIT OF RAGE, SAUL SETS OUT...

I'LL KILL HIM MYSELF! DAVID MAY BE A HERO TO THE PEOPLE, BUT HE WON'T LIVE TO TAKE MY KINGDOM FROM ME!

—BUT ON THE WAY A STRANGE THING HAPPENS...

GOD TAKES CONTROL OF SAUL. AND WHEN SAUL REACHES RAMAH HE FALLS TO THE GROUND AND LIES THERE FOR A DAY AND A NIGHT.

WHILE SAUL IS IN RAMAH, DAVID HURRIES BACK TO THE PALACE TO SEE HIS FRIEND, PRINCE JONATHAN

DAVID! WHAT BRINGS YOU BACK HERE?

I MUST KNOW WHY YOUR FATHER WANTS TO KILL ME. COME—LET'S GO WHERE WE CAN TALK WITHOUT BEING HEARD.

MY FATHER MEANS YOU NO HARM, DAVID. HE WOULD TELL ME IF HE DID.

NO, JONATHAN. HE WOULD NOT TELL YOU BECAUSE YOU ARE MY FRIEND.

TOMORROW STARTS THE KING'S FEAST OF THE NEW MOON—BUT I WON'T ATTEND. IF YOUR FATHER ASKS ABOUT ME, TELL HIM I HAVE GONE TO BETHLEHEM TO SEE MY FAMILY. IF HE IS NOT ANGRY, THEN ALL IS WELL. BUT IF HE IS—REMEMBER THE AGREEMENT WE MADE BEFORE GOD TO BE FRIENDS, ALWAYS.

I'LL FIND OUT THE TRUTH. NOW, LET'S GO OUT IN THE FIELD WHERE WE CAN SET UP A SECRET PLAN FOR ME TO LET YOU KNOW HOW MY FATHER FEELS.

AFRAID THAT DAVID WILL TAKE HIS KINGDOM FROM HIM, KING SAUL SETS OUT WITH HIS ARMY TO CAPTURE DAVID. ON THE WAY HE STOPS TO REST IN A CAVE—UNAWARE THAT DAVID AND HIS MEN ARE HIDING IN THE BACK OF IT.

WHY DOESN'T DAVID KILL HIM?

HE JUST STANDS THERE!

DAVID LOOKS DOWN AT THE KING—AND THINKS OF ALL THE TIMES SAUL HAS TRIED TO KILL HIM. NOW THE JEALOUS KING IS AT HIS MERCY—BUT DAVID ONLY BENDS DOWN AND CAREFULLY CUTS OFF A PIECE OF THE ROYAL ROBE.

HE'S YOUR WIFE'S FATHER—SO IF YOU DON'T WANT TO KILL HIM, I'LL DO IT FOR YOU.

NO—HE WAS CHOSEN BY GOD TO BE OUR KING. IT IS NOT FOR US TO DECIDE WHEN HE WILL DIE.

AFTER A TIME SAUL LEAVES THE CAVE—AND DAVID CALLS AFTER HIM.

MY LORD THE KING.

DAVID!

WHY DO YOU KEEP HUNTING ME? I MEAN YOU NO HARM. SEE THIS PIECE OF CLOTH? I CUT IT FROM YOUR ROBE. I COULD HAVE KILLED YOU, BUT I DIDN'T.

I AM ASHAMED. YOU ARE A BETTER MAN THAN I AM, DAVID. I WILL GO NOW AND LEAVE YOU ALONE.

SAUL LEADS HIS ARMY AWAY ...BUT A SHORT TIME LATER DAVID LEARNS THAT SAUL HAS FORCED MICHAL DAVID'S WIFE, TO MARRY ANOTHER MAN. DAVID KNOWS NOW THAT SAUL IS STILL ANGRY AND THAT HE WILL NEVER BE SAFE AS LONG AS SAUL LIVES. WORD COMES, TOO, THAT HIS OLD FRIEND, SAMUEL, THE PROPHET, IS DEAD.

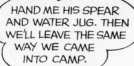

HAND ME HIS SPEAR AND WATER JUG. THEN WE'LL LEAVE THE SAME WAY WE CAME INTO CAMP.

THE NEXT MORNING DAVID CALLS DOWN TO SAUL'S CAMP.

KING SAUL! LOOK! I HAVE YOUR SPEAR AND WATER JUG!

YOU TOOK THEM WHILE I SLEPT! AGAIN YOU COULD HAVE KILLED ME— AND YOU DIDN'T. I HAVE BEEN A FOOL! I'LL NEVER TRY TO HARM YOU AGAIN.

ASHAMED, KING SAUL ORDERS HIS MEN TO BREAK CAMP AND RETURN HOME.

LOOK! THEY'RE LEAVING—YOU'RE SAFE!

NO—SAUL PROMISED THAT BEFORE. I'LL NEVER BE SAFE AS LONG AS THE KING LIVES.

AND I'M TIRED OF BEING HUNTED LIKE AN OUTLAW. I'M GOING BACK TO THE LAND OF THE PHILISTINES.

PHILISTINES! BUT, UNCLE DAVID, THEY'RE ENEMIES OF ISRAEL. THEY'LL KILL YOU ON SIGHT.

SO—FOR THE FIRST TIME SINCE THEY JOINED DAVID—HIS FOLLOWERS HAVE A SETTLED PLACE IN WHICH TO LIVE.

DAVID REASONS THAT THE PHILISTINES KNOW OF HIS TROUBLE WITH SAUL AND THAT THIS TIME THEY WILL ACCEPT HIM. AND HE IS RIGHT. KING ACHISH OF THE PHILISTINES IS GLAD TO HAVE DAVID'S SIX HUNDRED WARRIORS ON HIS SIDE. HE EVEN GIVES THEM THE CITY OF ZIKLAG TO LIVE IN.

IT'S GOOD, ABIGAIL, TO SEE MY MEN RAISING THEIR FAMILIES IN PEACE.

AND I'M SO GLAD YOUR LIFE IS NO LONGER IN DANGER.

ONE DAY DAVID SEES KING ACHISH RIDING INTO THE CITY.

I WONDER WHAT BRINGS HIM HERE?

I PRAY HIS VISIT IS A FRIENDLY ONE.

DAVID GOES OUT TO WELCOME THE KING.

GREETINGS, DAVID. WE ARE PLANNING AN ATTACK ON YOUR OLD ENEMY, KING SAUL, AND WE EXPECT YOU TO HELP US.

HOW CAN I FIGHT MY OWN PEOPLE? KING SAUL AND PRINCE JONATHAN WILL BE LEADING THE ISRAELITES!

At the Witch's House

FROM I SAMUEL 29; 28: 5-11

AND HE COULD CUT US TO PIECES WHILE WE'RE BUSY AT THE FRONT.

I THINK DAVID IS LOYAL TO ME. BUT, IF YOU WISH, I'LL SEND HIM HOME.

ACHISH CALLS FOR DAVID.

I FIND NO FAULT IN YOU, DAVID, BUT THE OTHERS DON'T TRUST YOU. YOU'D BETTER RETURN HOME AS SOON AS IT IS LIGHT.

DAVID'S PRAYER HAS BEEN ANSWERED. AT DAWN HE LEADS HIS SOLDIERS OUT OF THE CAMP AND BACK TOWARD THEIR CITY OF ZIKLAG. THE PHILISTINES MARCH ON...

WHEN SAUL SEES THE POWERFUL PHILISTINE ARMY, HE IS AFRAID. FRANTICALLY HE CALLS UPON GOD FOR HELP—BUT GOD DOES NOT ANSWER. TERRIFIED, HE CALLS FOR A SERVANT.

THEN SAUL HEARS THE VOICE OF SAMUEL: BECAUSE YOU DISOBEYED GOD, THE LORD WILL DELIVER ISRAEL INTO THE HANDS OF THE PHILISTINES. TOMORROW YOU AND YOUR SONS WILL BE DEAD.

On the Robbers' Trail

FROM 1 SAMUEL 30: 1-11

DAVID AND HIS MEN RETURN TO FIND THEIR CITY OF ZIKLAG IN SMOLDERING RUINS.

IN VAIN THEY SEARCH THROUGH THE RUBBLE AND ASHES FOR THEIR FAMILIES.

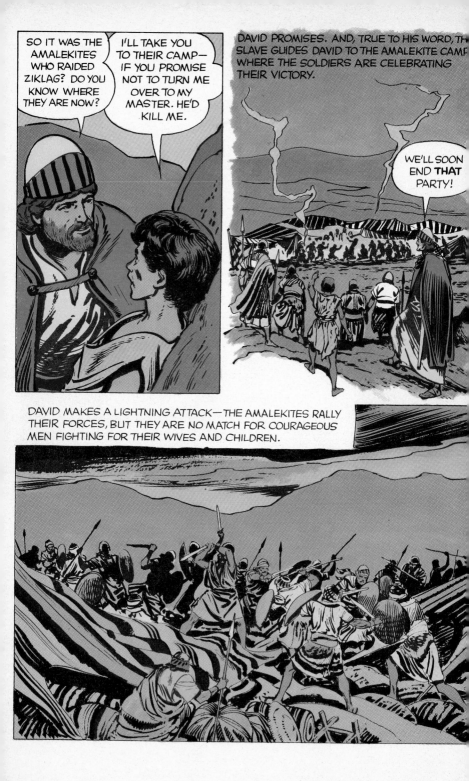

HOW DO YOU KNOW THIS?

I DO NOT KNOW HOW JONATHAN DIED, BUT I FOUND THE KING ON THE BATTLEFIELD. HE WAS INJURED, AND HE ASKED ME TO KILL HIM. I DID—AND HERE ARE HIS CROWN AND BRACELETS TO PROVE IT!

DAVID DOES NOT KNOW THAT THE MAN IS TELLING A LIE, WITH THE HOPE OF RECEIVING A REWARD. FOR A MOMENT HE IS LOST IN GRIEF—THEN HE TURNS IN ANGER UPON THE MAN WHO BROUGHT THE NEWS.

EVEN IF THE KING ASKED YOU TO KILL HIM, YOU HAD NO RIGHT TO TAKE THE LIFE OF THE MAN CHOSEN BY GOD TO BE KING OF ISRAEL. FOR THIS CRIME YOU WILL PAY—WITH YOUR LIFE!

SO THE MAN WHO LIED TO WIN FAVOR WITH DAVID LOSES NOT ONLY THE FAVOR—BUT HIS LIFE!

THEN, BEFORE ALL OF HIS FAITHFUL FOLLOWERS, DAVID SINGS A MEMORIAL SONG FOR JONATHAN AND THE KING.

Song of the Bow

...How are the mighty fallen!...
The bow of Jonathan turned not back,
And the sword of Saul returned not empty....
In their death they were not divided:
They were swifter than eagles,
They were stronger than lions....
I am distressed for thee, my brother Jonathan:
Very pleasant hast thou been unto me:
Thy love to me was wonderful,
Passing the love of women.
How are the mighty fallen,
And the weapons of war perished!

ABNER IS SCARCELY OUT OF THE CITY WHEN JOAB RETURNS...

ABNER JUST LEFT—DAVID HAD A BIG FEAST FOR HIM.

ABNER *HERE*? AND DAVID LET HIM GO?

ANGRILY JOAB RUSHES IN TO SEE DAVID...

DON'T YOU KNOW THAT ABNER CAME HERE AS A SPY—TO FIND OUT YOUR STRENGTH?

DAVID REFUSES TO LISTEN—AND IN A RAGE JOAB STORMS OUT.

I'LL HANDLE THIS *MY* WAY!

JOAB IS FURIOUS! THIS COULD MEAN TROUBLE!

HE WOULDN'T DARE DEFY THE KING!

WELCOME, ABNER. I HAVE AN IMPORTANT MATTER TO TAKE UP WITH YOU—WILL YOU STEP OVER HERE WHERE WE CAN TAKE IT UP QUIETLY?

GREETINGS, JOAB. OF COURSE.

JOAB LEADS ABNER TO A QUIET CORNER OF THE BUSY GATE. AND THERE, BEFORE ABNER CAN SUSPECT WHAT IS GOING ON—JOAB STABS HIM.

DAVID IS ANGRY WHEN HE LEARNS OF ABNER'S MURDER. HE CALLS THE PEOPLE TOGETHER AND ACCUSES JOAB.

THE PUNISHMENT OF JOAB IS IN THE HANDS OF GOD!

TO FURTHER SHOW HIS DISAPPROVAL FOR WHAT JOAB HAS DONE, DAVID LEADS THE MOURNERS IN ABNER'S FUNERAL PROCESSION. BUT EVEN AS KING, DAVID IS NOT SECURE ENOUGH IN HIS NEW KINGDOM TO PUNISH JOAB, FOR JOAB IS THE LEADER OF DAVID'S ARMY.

DAVID MOURNS THE DEATH OF ABNER, BUT ABNER'S MASTER, KING ISH-BOSHETH, IS SHAKEN WITH FRIGHT.

WHAT BAD NEWS! WITHOUT ABNER, I'M LOST.

KING ISH-BOSHETH'S FEARS ARE WELL GROUNDED FOR EVEN AS HE RECEIVES THE NEWS OF ABNER'S DEATH, TWO OF HIS OWN ARMY OFFICERS ARE PLOTTING...

WITHOUT ABNER, KING ISH-BOSHETH IS A WEAKLING. IF DAVID ATTACKS US, WE'LL BE WIPED OUT.

I HAVE AN IDE THAT COULD GIVE US POWE —AND A REWAR LISTEN—JUST THE TWO OF US..

WONDERFUL! LET'S DO IT NOW WHILE IT'S DARK.

NO—IT WILL BE EASIER IF WE JUST WALK INTO THE PALACE IN BROAD DAYLIGHT— AS IF WE WERE GETTING GRAIN. THEN NO ONE WOULD SUSPECT.

AT NOON THE NEXT DAY, WHILE THE KING IS TAKING HIS NAP...

THE REWARD WILL SOON BE OURS!

Hail to the King!

ROM 2 SAMUEL 4: 6—5: 4

THE WAR AGAINST KING DAVID LEAVES KING ISH-BOSHETH WITH FEW LOYAL FOLLOWERS. IN BROAD DAYLIGHT TWO OF HIS OWN OFFICERS ENTER THE KING'S PALACE...

THE KING'S ROOM IS DOWN THIS HALL.

HE IS ASLEEP.

GOOD—BUT WE MUST ACT SWIFTLY!

BOLDLY THE MEN ENTER THE KING'S BEDROOM AND—WHILE THE PALACE IS RESTING DURING THE HEAT OF THE DAY—THEY KILL HIM. THEN...

QUIETLY, SO THAT NO ONE WILL SUSPECT THEIR ERRAND...THEY WALK OUT OF THE PALACE AND INTO THE STREET. NIGHT FINDS THEM TRAVELING DOWN THE PLAIN TOWARD DAVID'S CAPITAL IN HEBRON.

BEFORE DAVID THEY PROUDLY TELL THEIR STORY.

WE BRING GOOD NEWS, O KING. **WE** HAVE KILLED YOUR ENEMY, KING ISH-BOSHETH!

WE THOUGHT SOME REWARD...

REWARD! DO YOU THINK I WILL REWARD YOU FOR KILLING AN INNOCENT MAN? THERE'S NO ROOM IN MY KINGDOM FOR TRAITORS WHO BETRAY THEIR KING! GUARDS! TAKE THEM AWAY—EXECUTE THEM.

Underground Attack

FROM 2 SAMUEL 5: 5-9

SURPRISED BY THE SUDDEN APPEARANCE OF DAVID'S MEN, THE GUARDS ARE QUICKLY OVERCOME.

GIVE THE ORDER TO OPEN THE GATES— OR DIE!

THE TERRIFIED OFFICER SHOUTS THE ORDER. THE HUGE GATES SWING OPEN...

AND DAVID'S ARMY CHARGES THROUGH.

BUT ONE DAY DAVID LOOKS AT THE TENT AND CALLS NATHAN, THE PROPHET OF GOD, TO HIM.

IT ISN'T RIGHT FOR GOD'S HOUSE TO BE A TENT WHILE I LIVE IN A PALACE. I'D LIKE TO BUILD A TEMPLE TO GOD.

I'M SURE GOD WOULD BE PLEASED.

THAT NIGHT GOD SPEAKS TO NATHAN— AND THE NEXT DAY NATHAN TELLS DAVID THAT GOD DOES NOT WANT HIM TO BUILD THE TEMPLE. DAVID IS A MAN OF WAR, AND THE TEMPLE IS TO BE BUILT BY A MAN OF PEACE. GOD PROMISES TO GIVE DAVID A SON WHO WILL BUILD A HOUSE FOR GOD

THEN DAVID REMEMBERS A PROMISE HE HIMSELF MADE YEARS BEFORE TO HIS BEST FRIEND, JONATHAN. EACH HAD VOWED TO BE KIND TO THE OTHER'S CHILDREN. DAVID INQUIRES ABOUT JONATHAN'S FAMILY.

SEND FOR HIM.

REMEMBER, HE IS ALSO KING SAUL'S GRANDSON. BUT FOR YOU HE MIGHT BE SITTING ON THE THRONE OF ISRAEL. HE MAY HATE YOU...

YES, PRINCE JONATHAN HAD A SON, MEPHIBOSHETH.

A King Is Tempted

FROM 2 SAMUEL 9: 6—11: 14

DAVID ORDERS JONATHAN'S SON BROUGHT TO HIM. BUT HE IS SHOCKED WHEN MEPHIBOSHETH APPEARS -- A CRIPPLE.

HAVE MERCY ON YOUR SERVANT AND HIS CHILD, O KING.

MERCY? WHY DO YO ASK FOR MERCY?

I AM THE GRANDSON OF YOUR ENEMY, KING SAUL. DID YOU NOT SEND FOR ME TO PUT ME TO DEATH?

NO, MEPHIBOSHETH -- NO! I SENT FOR YOU BECAUSE I LOVED YOUR FATHER, JONATHAN. I DID NOT KNOW YOU WERE LAME.

I WAS ONLY FIVE WHEN THE NEWS OF MY FATHER'S DEATH CAME. AS MY NURSE RAN IN FRIGHT, SHE DROPPED ME. I HAVE BEEN CRIPPLED EVER SINCE.

I AM SORRY -- AND I REGRET THAT YOUR GRANDFATHER'S LAND WAS NOT RESTORED TO YOU BEFORE. IT IS NOW YOURS -- AND I INVITE YOU TO EAT EVERY DAY AT MY TABLE.

I AM GRATEFUL FOR YOUR KINDNESS.

AND I THANK GOD I AM ABLE TO KEEP MY PROMISE TO YOUR FATHER.

UNDER DAVID'S LEADERSHIP, ISRAEL GROWS STRONGER EVERY DAY. BUT RULERS OF THE COUNTRIES AROUND GROW WORRIED.

WORD HAS COME THAT THE SYRIANS AND AMMONITES ARE JOINING FORCES AGAINST US.

I CAN'T LEAVE JERUSALEM NOW, JOAB. CALL UP THE ARMY AND GO OUT TO MEET THEM.

JOAB TAKES CHARGE OF THE WAR. ABOUT A YEAR LATER, AS DAVID STROLLS ON THE ROOF OF HIS PALACE...

WHO IS THAT BEAUTIFUL WOMAN?

BATH-SHEBA, THE WIFE OF URIAH, A SOLDIER IN YOUR ARMY.

DAVID SENDS A MESSENGER TO BRING BATH-SHEBA TO HIS COURT.

YOU SENT FOR ME, O KING?

SHE IS EVEN MORE BEAUTIFUL THAN I THOUGHT!

IF ONLY I COULD MARRY HER! THE PROBLEM IS URIAH IS HER HUSBAN

BUT SOLDIERS SOMETIMES DIE IN BATTLE. THAT'S IT!

THINKING ONLY OF HIS LOVE FOR BATH-SHE DAVID SENDS FOR URIAH ON THE EXCUSE O ASKING ABOUT THE WAR.

THE ENEMY IS STRONG. BUT JOAB THINKS WE CAN FORCE THEIR SURRENDER SOON.

I AM SURE OF IT. PREPARE TO RETURI TO THE FRONT--ANI TAKE THIS MESSAGE TO JOAB.

King David's Sin

URIAH, THE HUSBAND OF BATH-SHEBA, RETURNS TO THE BATTLEFRONT WITH A MESSAGE FROM KING DAVID TO JOAB, GENERAL OF THE ISRAELITE FORCES.

... AND SENDS WORD TO DAVID.

WE FOUGHT BRAVELY-- BUT THE ARCHERS ON THE CITY WALLS HAD THE ADVANTAGE. URIAH, THE LEADER OF THE ATTACK, WAS KILLED.

TELL JOAB NOT TO FEEL BADLY -- WAR ALWAYS TAKES SOME OF OUR BEST MEN. STEP UP THE ATTACK AND TAKE THE CITY.

ACROSS THE CITY, BATH-SHEBA MOURNS FOR HER HUSBAND -- BUT IN HER HEART SHE KNOWS THAT NOW SHE IS FREE TO MARRY THE KING.

WHEN BATH-SHEBA'S TIME OF MOURNING IS OVER, DAVID CALLS HER TO THE PALACE, AND THEY ARE MARRIED.

LONG LIVE THE KING! LONG LIVE THE QUEEN!

LATER, WHEN A SON IS BORN TO BATH-SHEBA, THE KING AND ALL ISRAEL REJOICE... BUT GOD IS NOT PLEASED! EVEN WHILE THE PEOPLE SHOUT THEIR PRAISES, A MAN OF GOD IS ON HIS WAY TO THE PALACE...

The King's Punishment

FROM 2 SAMUEL 12: 1-14

DAVID HAS MARRIED THE BEAUTIFUL BATH-SHEBA. WHEN THEIR SON IS BORN, DAVID IS PROUD AND HAPPY UNTIL ONE DAY... NATHAN, THE PROPHET OF GOD, COMES TO SEE HIM.

WELCOME, NATHAN. WHAT CAN I DO FOR YOU?

I HAVE COME TO TELL YOU ABOUT A GREAT INJUSTICE THAT HAS BEEN DONE IN YOUR KINGDOM.

INJUSTICE IN **MY** KINGDOM? TELL ME ABOUT IT.

THERE WERE TWO MEN IN A CITY...

ONE WAS RICH, THE OTHER POOR. THE RICH MAN HAD MANY FLOCKS, BUT THE POOR MAN HAD ONLY ONE LITTLE LAMB WHICH HE LOVED DEARLY.

ONE DAY THE RICH MAN HAD A GUEST. HE TOOK THE LAMB FROM THE POOR MAN AND HAD IT KILLED TO SERVE FOR THE FEAST.

DURING THE TELLING OF THE STORY DAVID'S ANGER MOUNTS...

A MAN WHO WOULD DO THAT SHOULD BE PUT TO DEATH!

YOU, O KING, ARE THAT MAN! GOD MADE YOU RICH AND POWERFUL. BUT YOU WANTED BATH-SHEBA, THE WIFE OF ONE OF YOUR MOST LOYAL SOLDIERS. YOU HAD HIM KILLED SO THAT YOU MIGHT MARRY HER--JUST AS THE RICH MAN TOOK THE POOR MAN'S LAMB!

I HAVE SINNED! I HAVE SINNED AGAINST THE LORD!

AND YOUR SIN WILL BRING TROUBLE TO YOU AND YOUR FAMILY. THE CHILD WHICH HAS BEEN BORN TO YOU AND BATH-SHEBA WILL DIE!

NO, NATHAN! NOT MY CHILD!

HE'S GONE!

MEANWHILE JOAB, DAVID'S GENERAL, CONTINUES THE SIEGE AGAINST THE CITY OF RABBAH. TO HONOR DAVID, HE SENDS WORD FOR THE KING TO COME AND MAKE THE FINAL ATTACK. DAVID LEADS THE CHARGE -- AND THE CITY SURRENDERS.

RETURNING VICTORIOUS INTO JERUSALEM, DAVID IS GREETED WITH SHOUTS OF PRAISE. HE IS PLEASED AND PROUD -- ISRAEL IS STRONG, AND NO NATION WOULD DARE ATTACK IT, BUT...

DAVID DOES NOT REALIZE THAT TROUBLE BUILDING UP WITHIN HIS OWN PALACE WALLS WILL ENDANGER HIS THRONE.

SOON AFTER DAVID'S TRIUMPHAL RETURN, PRINCE ABSALOM MAKES A SPECIAL VISIT TO HIS FATHER.

IT'S SHEEPSHEARING TIME, AND I'M HAVING A BIG FEAST IN THE COUNTRY. WILL YOU HONOR MY GUESTS WITH YOUR PRESENCE?

THANK YOU, ABSALOM, BUT IF YOU ARE HAVING A BIG FEAST, I DON'T WANT TO ADD TO YOUR EXPENSES.

THEN MAY MY [BR]OTHERS COME? [P]RINCE AMNON CAN [R]EPRESENT YOU.

AMNON? I THOUGHT ABSALOM HATED HIM.

YES, I'M PLEASED THAT YOU WANT TO HONOR YOUR BROTHERS THIS WAY.

ABSALOM DOES HATE HIS OLDER HALF-BROTHER, AMNON, WHO HAS FIRST RIGHT TO DAVID'S THRONE. WHEN AMNON ACCEPTS THE INVITATION, ABSALOM CALLS IN HIS SERVANTS.

AMNON IS COMING TO THE FEAST. WHEN I GIVE THE WORD -- KILL HIM!

AT THE HEIGHT OF THE FEAST, AMNON IS KILLED... AFRAID FOR THEIR LIVES, THE REST OF THE BROTHERS FLEE INTO THE NIGHT...

A Prince's Command!

FROM 2 SAMUEL 13: 30—14: 30

MESSENGERS BRING WORD TO THE PALACE IN JERUSALEM THAT KING DAVID'S SON, ABSALOM, HAS KILLED ALL OF HIS BROTHERS. STUNNED BY SHOCK AND GRIEF, DAVID FALLS TO THE GROUND--WEEPING. BUT HIGH ON THE CITY WALLS THE MAN IN THE TOWER KEEPS WATCH...

LOOK! A BAND OF MEN RIDING THIS WAY!

THE MEN ARE DAVID'S SONS AND THEIR SERVANTS.

FULL SPEED THEY
PE INTO THE CITY
D RUSH TO THEIR
THER.

MY SONS! THEY TOLD ME YOU WERE ALL KILLED! WHAT HAPPENED?

ABSALOM MURDERED AMNON -- THE REST OF US ESCAPED!

THANK GOD, YOU ARE AFE -- BUT AMNON, MY RST-BORN IS DEAD! ILLED BY HIS OWN BROTHER! WHERE S ABSALOM NOW?

HE FLED -- WE THINK HE WENT TO GESHUR.

FOR THREE YEARS DAVID GRIEVES FOR THE SON WHO RAN AWAY. FINALLY HE SENDS HIS GENERAL, JOAB, TO ABSALOM.

YOUR FATHER MISSES YOU, ABSALOM. HE HAS SENT ME TO BRING YOU BACK TO JERUSALEM.

I'M GLAD HE'S FORGIVEN ME.

HE HASN'T ENTIRELY FORGIVEN YOU, ABSALOM. HE SAYS YOU CAN'T LIVE IN THE PALACE OR COME TO SEE HIM.

IF THAT'S THE WAY HE WANTS IT, ALL RIGHT.

HE WON... TREAT M... THIS W... FOR LON...

FOR TWO YEARS ABSALOM LIVES IN JERUSALEM WITHOUT SEEING HIS FATHER. HE RESENTS THIS TREATMENT AND HIS ANGER GROWS UNTIL AT LAST HE CAN STAND IT NO LONGER. HE SENDS FOR JOAB. JOAB REFUSES TO COME. ABSALOM SENDS A SECOND TIME.

JOAB STILL WON'T COME, SIR.

OH, YES HE WILL-- AND IN A HURRY!

JOAB HAS A BARLEY FIELD NEXT TO MINE. SET FIRE TO IT!

I'M A PRINCE, AND I SHOULD BE TREATED LIKE MY BROTHERS. GO TO MY FATHER AND ASK HIM IF HE WILL SEE ME.

BUT... HE ASKED ME TO COME BACK TO JERUSALEM. IF HE WANTS TO PUNISH ME FOR WHAT I DI[D] LET HIM DO IT. IF NOT, THEN LET HIM TREAT ME LIKE A SON AGAIN.

JOAB CARRIES ABSALOM'S MESSAGE TO KING DAVID.

YOUR SON MISSES YOU – HE WISHES TO BE FORGIVEN AND WELCOMED BACK INTO THE FAMILY.

HE MISSES ME? NO MORE THAN I MISS HIM. TELL HIM TO COME TO ME.

ABSALOM PRETENDS TO BE HUMBLE AS H[E] BOWS BEFORE HIS FATHER--ASKING FORGIV[E]NESS. BUT IN HIS HEART HE HAS AN EVIL PLA[N]

RISE UP, ABSALOM. YOU ARE FORGIVEN. FROM NOW ON YOU WILL BE WELCOME AT THE PALACE AS A PRINCE OF ISRAEL.

Revolt!

FROM 2 SAMUEL 15: 7-13

FOR SEVERAL YEARS ABSALOM CARRIES ON A CAMPAIGN TO GAIN FOLLOWERS SO THAT HE CAN OVERTHROW HIS FATHER'S KINGDOM. AT LAST THE TIME IS RIPE FOR HIS FINAL MOVE... HE GOES TO HIS FATHER...

AFTER I KILLED MY BROTHER AND WAS LIVING IN GESHUR, I MADE A VOW THAT IF I COULD RETURN AGAIN TO JERUSALEM, I WOULD SERVE THE LORD. MAY I GO TO MY BIRTHPLACE, HEBRON, TO OFFER A SACRIFICE TO GOD?

YOU HAVE MY PERMISSION, SON, AND MY BLESSING.

THE NEWS THAT HIS OWN SON, ABSALOM, HAS LED A REVOLT AGAINST HIM LEAVES DAVID IN A STATE OF SHOCK.

ABSALOM! HOW CAN I FIGHT MY OWN SON--MY OWN PEOPLE? WHOM CAN I COUNT ON TO STAND WITH ME?

YOUR FRIENDS WILL MAKE THEMSELVES KNOWN.

WE MUST ESCAPE BEFORE ABSALOM ATTACKS THE CITY! TELL MY FAMILY-- MY SERVANTS -- ALL WHO ARE LOYAL--TO GET READY TO LEAVE JERUSALEM!

AT DAWN DAVID LEADS HIS PEOPLE OUT OF THE CITY--AT THE LAST HOUSE HE STOPS TO WATCH HIS FOLLOWERS PASS BY.

IN THE PROCESSION ARE THE PRIES CARRYING GOD'S HOLY ARK.

STOP--TAKE IT BACK TO THE CITY. IF GOD WILLS IT, I WILL RETURN TO THE CITY AND WORSHIP AGAIN BEFORE HIS ARK.

THE NUMBER WHO CHOOSE TO JOIN DAVID GROWS WITH EACH PASSING HOUR. BUT DAVID SENDS ONE OF THEM BACK...

HUSHAI, YOU CAN SERVE ME BETTER IF YOU OFFER TO HELP ABSALOM. MAYBE YOU CAN KEEP HIM FROM FOLLOWING THE ADVICE OF THOSE WHO HAVE BETRAYED ME.

YOU ARE MY KING, AND I WILL SERVE IN ANY WAY YOU ASK.

HUSHAI RETURNS -- IN TIME TO SEE ABSALOM RIDE INTO THE CITY. IN THE CROWDS THERE ARE SHOUTS OF JOY AND PRAISE -- BUT THERE IS ALSO FEAR...

THIS MEANS WAR!

LIKE THE MAN IN THE CROWD, HUSHAI KNOWS THAT WAR WILL SOON BE UPON THEM. HE OFFERS HIS SERVICES TO ABSALOM -- AND ALONG WITH AHITHOPHEL IS CALLED TO THE FIRST COUNCIL OF WAR. AHITHOPHEL SPEAKS FIRST.

WE MUST ATTACK WHILE DAVID IS WEAK AND ON THE RUN.

NO, AHITHOPHEL'S ADVICE IS NOT GOOD. DAVID AND HIS MEN ARE ISRAEL'S BEST FIGHTERS. AND RIGHT NOW THEY ARE ANGRY AS BEARS ROBBED OF THEIR YOUNG. IF YOU ATTACK AND SUFFER ANY DEFEAT, THE PEOPLE WILL TURN AGAINST YOU. WAIT UNTIL YOU CAN CALL UP THOUSANDS OF MEN... THEN IF YOU, O KING, LEAD THEM...

Hide-out in a Well

FROM 2 SAMUEL 17: 14-23

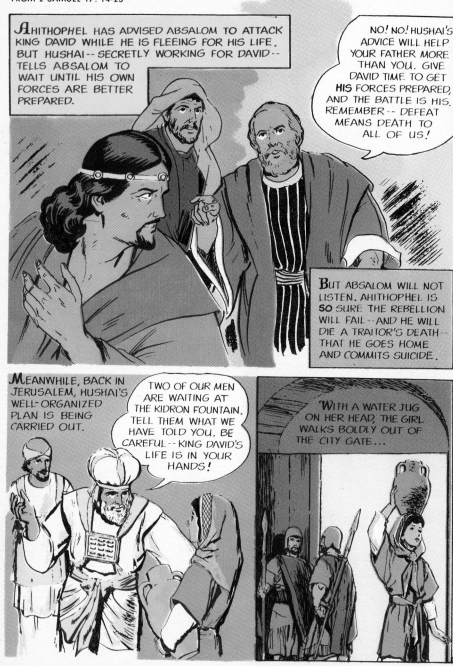

AHITHOPHEL HAS ADVISED ABSALOM TO ATTACK KING DAVID WHILE HE IS FLEEING FOR HIS LIFE. BUT HUSHAI--SECRETLY WORKING FOR DAVID-- TELLS ABSALOM TO WAIT UNTIL HIS OWN FORCES ARE BETTER PREPARED.

NO! NO! HUSHAI'S ADVICE WILL HELP YOUR FATHER MORE THAN YOU. GIVE DAVID TIME TO GET HIS FORCES PREPARED, AND THE BATTLE IS HIS. REMEMBER -- DEFEAT MEANS DEATH TO ALL OF US!

BUT ABSALOM WILL NOT LISTEN. AHITHOPHEL IS SO SURE THE REBELLION WILL FAIL--AND HE WILL DIE A TRAITOR'S DEATH-- THAT HE GOES HOME AND COMMITS SUICIDE.

MEANWHILE, BACK IN JERUSALEM, HUSHAI'S WELL-ORGANIZED PLAN IS BEING CARRIED OUT.

TWO OF OUR MEN ARE WAITING AT THE KIDRON FOUNTAIN. TELL THEM WHAT WE HAVE TOLD YOU. BE CAREFUL--KING DAVID'S LIFE IS IN YOUR HANDS!

WITH A WATER JUG ON HER HEAD, THE GIRL WALKS BOLDLY OUT OF THE CITY GATE...

AND AT THE APPOINTED PLACE MEETS THE TWO MEN.

TELL KING DAVID NOT TO STOP UNTIL HE HAS REACHED THE OTHER SIDE OF THE JORDAN RIVER.

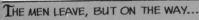

THE MEN LEAVE, BUT ON THE WAY...

DON'T LOOK NOW, BUT I THINK WE HAVE BEEN SEEN. LET'S PLAY IT SAFE AND HIDE OUT IN BAHURIM.

SPIES!

THE BOY RACES BACK TO THE CITY AND REPORTS WHAT HE HAS SEEN TO PRINCE ABSALOM.

FIND THOSE SPIES AND BRING THEM TO ME!

ABSALOM'S SOLDIERS FOLLOW THE TRAIL UNTIL THEY REACH A HOUSE IN BAHURIM...

WE'RE SEARCHING FOR SPIES...HAS ANYONE BEEN HERE?

YES, TWO MEN. BUT THEY LEFT-- IN THE DIRECTION OF THE RIVER.

THE SOLDIERS SEARCH THE HOUSE BUT WHEN THEY FIND NOTHING, THE MOVE ON.

COME UP--THE SOLDIER HAVE GONE.

EVEN ABSALOM'S MEN WOULDN'T KNOW THERE WAS A WELL HERE. I'M GLAD IT WAS A DRY ONE.

I'M PROUD TO HELP MY KING, BUT--GO-- THE SOLDIERS MIGHT RETURN.

THE MESSENGERS HURRY ON... AND THAT NIGHT DAVID AND HIS FOLLOWERS CROSS OVER THE JORDAN.

ather Against Son

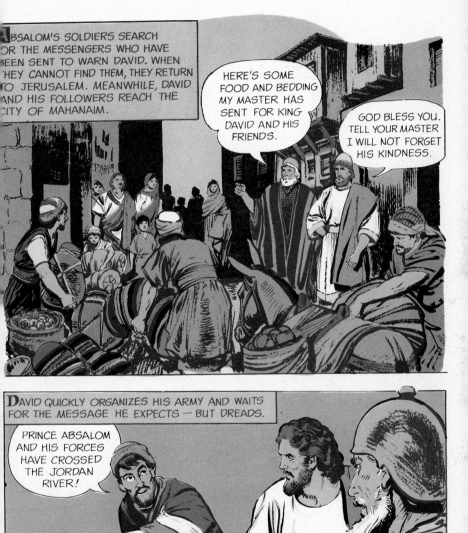

GOOD -- IF **WE** MOVE FAST WE CAN DETERMINE THE PLACE OF THE BATTLE.

RIGHT, JOAB. GIVE THE ORDERS TO MARCH. I'LL GO WITH YOU.

NO! YOUR LIFE IS TOO VALUABLE. STAY IN THE CITY AND BE READY TO SEND HELP IF WE NEED IT.

IF IT SEEMS BEST TO YOU I WILL STAY HERE.

AT THE GATE...

FOR MY SAKE, DEAL GENTLY WITH ABSALOM. HE'S MY SON, AND IN SPITE OF WHAT HE IS DOING, I LOVE HIM.

THE ARMIES MEET HEAD-ON THE WOODS OF EPHRAIM. AVID'S MEN ATTACK WITH UCH FURY THAT ABSALOM'S RMY IS THROWN INTO PANIC . AND RETREATS.

HE BATTLE IS LOST. ABSALOM IS FRAID THAT IF HE IS CAUGHT HE WILL UFFER A TRAITOR'S DEATH. HE TRIES O ESCAPE...

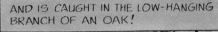

AND IS CAUGHT IN THE LOW-HANGING BRANCH OF AN OAK!

The King Returns

FROM 2 SAMUEL 18--24; 1 KINGS 1:1-9

PRINCE ABSALOM'S REVOLT AGAINST HIS FATHER, KING DAVID, LEADS TO A TERRIBLE BATTLE IN THE WOODS OF EPHRAIM. WHEN ABSALOM SEES THAT THE FIGHT IS GOING AGAINST HIM, HE TRIES TO ESCAPE, BUT...

GENERAL JOAB! ABSALOM IS CAUGHT-- BACK THERE-- IN A TREE!

ABSALOM? WHY DIDN'T YOU KILL HIM ON THE SPOT!

KILL THE KING'S SON? NEVER! I HEARD DAVID TELL YOU AND THE OTHER LEADERS TO BE CAREFUL OF ABSALOM.

WE'RE WASTING TIME-- I'LL DO IT MYSELF!

JOAB AND HIS ARMOR-BEARERS RUSH BACK TO THE TREE AND KILL ABSALOM. THE TRUMPET OF VICTORY IS SOUNDED-- THE BATTLE IS OVER!

MESSENGERS CARRY NEWS OF THE BATTLE TO DAVID.

MY SON, ABSALOM. IS HE ALL RIGHT?

MAY ALL THE KING'S ENEMIES BE AS THAT YOUNG MAN!

BROKENHEARTED, DAVID CLIMBS TO THE LOOKOUT ABOVE THE GATE. ALONE, HE MOURNS FOR HIS SON.

O MY SON ABSALOM. WOULD I HAD DIED INSTEAD OF YOU. MY SON! MY SON!

IN HIS GRIEF DAVID TURNS HIS BACK ON THE MEN WHO WON THE VICTORY FOR HIM. FINALLY JOAB GOES TO SEE THE KING.

YOU ACT AS IF YOU WISH ABSALOM HAD WON THE VICTORY! HAVE YOU FORGOTTEN THE MEN WHO FOUGHT TO SAVE YOU-- YOUR FAMILY--AND YOUR KINGDOM? IF THIS KEEPS UP, ALL YOUR FRIENDS WILL TURN AGAINST YOU!

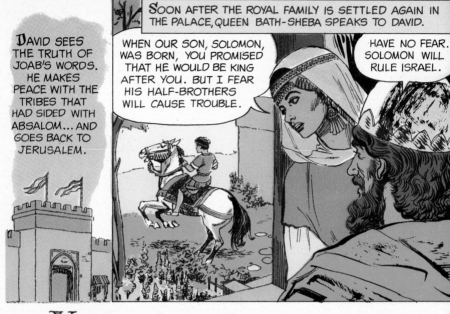

DAVID SEES THE TRUTH OF JOAB'S WORDS. HE MAKES PEACE WITH THE TRIBES THAT HAD SIDED WITH ABSALOM... AND GOES BACK TO JERUSALEM.

SOON AFTER THE ROYAL FAMILY IS SETTLED AGAIN IN THE PALACE, QUEEN BATH-SHEBA SPEAKS TO DAVID.

WHEN OUR SON, SOLOMON, WAS BORN, YOU PROMISED THAT HE WOULD BE KING AFTER YOU. BUT I FEAR HIS HALF-BROTHERS WILL CAUSE TROUBLE.

HAVE NO FEAR. SOLOMON WILL RULE ISRAEL.

YEARS PASS -- AND DAVID GROWS OLD. FINALLY WORD SPREADS THROUGHOUT JERUSALEM THAT THE KING'S HEALTH IS FAILING FAST. THE PEOPLE KNOW THAT DAVID HAS CHOSEN SOLOMON TO BE KING AND TO BUILD THE TEMPLE OF GOD. BUT THERE ARE RUMORS...

AND IN THE PALACE, ONE OF DAVID'S SONS, ADONIJAH, MEETS WITH THE HIGH PRIEST, ABIATHAR, AND GENERAL JOAB.

MY FATHER IS GROWING WEAKER -- AND THE TIME HAS COME FOR ME TO CARRY OUT OUR PLAN. BRING ALL THE KING'S SONS -- EXCEPT MY HALF-BROTHER SOLOMON — AND MEET ME AT THE SERPENT'S STONE.

FOLLOWING NATHAN'S ADVICE, SHE GOES AT ONCE TO DAVID.

MY LORD, YOU PROMISED THAT MY SON SOLOMON WOULD RULE AFTER YOU—BUT EVEN NOW HIS HALF-BROTHER, ADONIJAH, HAS DECLARED HIMSELF KING.

SEND FOR NATHAN AND ZADOK, THE PRIEST.

TAKE SOLOMON TO THE SACRED SPRING OF GIHON AND DECLARE HIM KING.

ZADOK AND NATHAN ACT AT ONCE... SOLOMON RIDES HIS FATHER'S MULE TO THE SPRING OF GIHON...

AND THERE HE IS MADE KING OF ISRAEL. THE TRUMPET SOUNDS...

GOD SAVE KING SOLOMON!

As SOLOMON RETURNS TO THE CITY, THE PEOPLE GREET THEIR NEW KING WITH SHOUTS OF JOY.

SO GREAT IS THE NOISE OF THE CELEBRATION THAT IT REACHES ADONIJAH'S FEAST.

WHAT'S GOING ON IN THE CITY?

AT THAT MOMENT A MESSENGER ENTERS...

WHAT GOOD NEWS DO YOU HAVE FOR US?

THE NOISE YOU HEAR IS THE SHOUTING OF ALL JERUSALEM! DAVID HAS MADE SOLOMON KING.

KNOWING THAT THEY MAY BE BRANDED AS TRAITORS, ADONIJAH'S GUESTS FLEE IN TERROR.

THERE'S ONLY ONE CHANCE TO SAVE MY LIFE.

Death of a King

FROM 1 KINGS 1: 49—2: 46

WHEN PRINCE ADONIJAH LEARNS THAT HIS FATHER, KING DAVID, HAS MADE SOLOMON KING OF ALL ISRAEL, ADONIJAH KNOWS THAT HIS OWN PLOT TO STEAL THE THRONE HAS FAILED. IN FEAR FOR HIS LIFE, HE RUNS TO THE TABERNACLE AND GRABS HOLD OF THE HORNS ON THE ALTAR OF SACRIFICE.

I WILL NOT LET GO UNTIL SOLOMON PROMISES NOT TO KILL ME.

SOLOMON AGREES TO SPARE ADONIJAH'S LIFE **IF** HE PROVES HIMSELF WORTHY OF THE KING'S TRUST. ADONIJAH PROMISES AND IS BROUGHT BEFORE HIS YOUNG HALF-BROTHER.

MY LORD AND KING!

SOLOMON LATER BELIEVES BOTH ADONIJAH AND GENERAL JOAB TO BE DISLOYAL, AND THEY ARE EXECUTED.

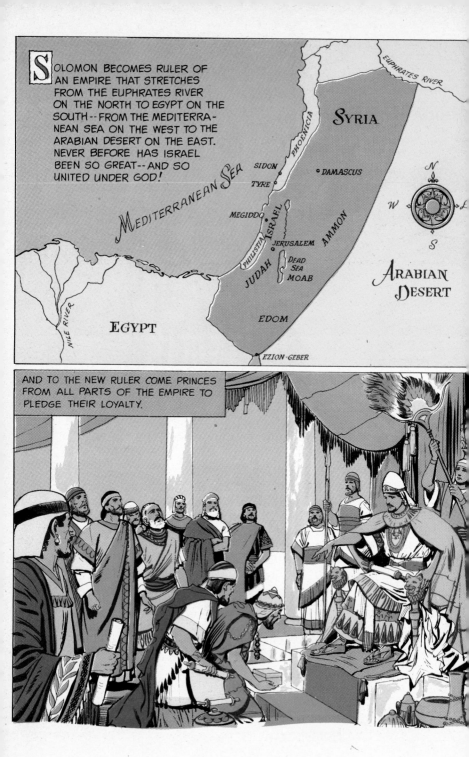

THE PEOPLE ARE HAPPY. ISRAEL IS AT PEACE. SOLOMON ESTABLISHES GOOD RELATIONS WITH MANY OF THE NEIGHBORING COUNTRIES BY MARRYING PRINCESSES OF THOSE NATIONS. RULERS OF THE COUNTRIES CONQUERED BY DAVID PAY TRIBUTE MONEY TO SOLOMON'S TREASURY. SO BEGINS THE GOLDEN AGE OF ISRAEL.

TO LAUNCH HIS FIRST GREAT BUILDING PROJECT, SOLOMON SENDS A MESSENGER TO HIS FATHER'S OLD FRIEND, KING HIRAM OF TYRE.

KING SOLOMON SENDS HIS GREETINGS--AND ASKS IF YOU WILL SEND HIM CEDAR AND CYPRESS LOGS AND SKILLED WORKERS TO HELP HIM BUILD A TEMPLE TO GOD IN JERUSALEM.

BLESSED BE THE LORD FOR GIVING MY FRIEND DAVID SUCH A WISE SON. TELL YOUR KING I WILL GIVE HIM WHAT HE ASKS IN EXCHANGE FOR WHEAT AND OIL, WHICH ARE SCARCE IN OUR COUNTRY.

THE DEAL IS MADE--AND SOON MEN BY THE THOUSANDS ARE ORDERED TO WORK IN THE FORESTS OF LEBANON, CUTTING CEDAR TREES FOR SOLOMON'S TEMPLE.

ON THE SEACOAST WEST OF THE LEBANON FORESTS THE LOGS ARE TIED TOGETHER TO FORM GIANT RAFTS. THESE ARE FLOATED DOWN TO ISRAEL.

AT THE SEAPORT OF JOPPA THE LOG RAFTS ARE BROKEN UP, AND THE TIMBERS ARE DRAGGED MORE THAN THIRTY MILES ACROSS RUGGED COUNTRY TO JERUSALEM.

NEAR JERUSALEM, THOUSANDS OF MEN TOIL IN THE GREAT QUARRIES.

CHISEL A BIT FROM THIS SIDE. EVERY STONE MUST BE MADE TO FIT PERFECTLY.

MEANWHILE, WOOD CARVERS AND GOLDBEATERS ARE AT WORK IN JERUSALEM.

THESE DOORS WOULD BE BEAUTIFUL JUST AS THEY ARE.

COVERED WITH GOLD, THEY'LL BE THE FINEST IN THE WORLD.

SLOWLY, CAREFULLY, FOR SEVEN LONG YEARS THE WORK GOES ON, UNTIL AT LAST, THE MOST BEAUTIFUL BUILDING IN ALL ISRAEL IS FINISHED...

The Temple of God

AFTER SEVEN LONG YEARS OF HARD WORK, THE MAGNIFICENT TEMPLE OF GOD IS COMPLETED. MEN, WOMEN, AND CHILDREN FROM ALL CORNERS OF ISRAEL CROWD INTO JERUSALEM TO WATCH THE PRIESTS CARRY THE SACRED ARK INTO THE TEMPLE. INSIDE, IN THE HOLY OF HOLIES-- A DARK, WINDOWLESS, HEAVILY CURTAINED ROOM-- THE ARK IS CAREFULLY PLACED BENEATH THE PROTECTING WINGS OF TWO FIFTEEN-FOOT GOLDEN CHERUBIM.

HORSES! BETWEEN FEEDING HIS FOREIGN WIVES, HIS SERVANTS, AND HIS HORSES, THERE'S LITTLE LEFT FOR THE POOR-- LIKE US!

STILL THE BUILDING PLANS GO ON...

OUR CARAVANS TRAVEL NORTH, SOUTH, EAST, AND WEST-- BUT WE HAVE MISSED ONE VITAL TRADE ROUTE.

WHERE?

THE SEA! I HAVE DECIDED TO BUILD MERCHANT SHIPS TO SAIL BEYOND THE RED SEA!

THE FLEET IS BUILT. ITS SHIPS BRING TREASURES INTO JERUSALEM AND CARRY AWAY WITH THEM STORIES OF THE CITY'S BEAUTY AND THE RULER'S WISDOM. THE STORIES REACH FAR AND WIDE — EVEN TO THE KINGDOM OF SHEBA IN THE ARABIAN PENINSULA.

SOLOMON! SOLOMON! ALL I HEAR ARE TALES OF HIS WEALTH AND WISDOM. I'M GOING TO JERUSALEM AND FIND OUT FOR MYSELF WHETHER THEY ARE TRUE!

A Queen's Visit

From I KINGS 10: 2—11: 8.

THE FAME OF SOLOMON'S WEALTH AND WISDOM SPREADS FAR AND WIDE. IN THE ARABIAN PENINSULA, THE QUEEN OF SHEBA IS SO CURIOUS THAT SHE SETS OUT ON A TRIP TO JERUSALEM TO SEE FOR HERSELF WHETHER THE STORIES ARE TRUE.

JERUSALEM HAS OUTGROWN ITS OLD WALLS OF DEFENSE, SO WE ARE BUILDING NEW ONES.

THAT FORE[MAN] SEEM[S] TO KNOW WH[AT] HE IS DOIN[G]

HOW OBSERVING YOU ARE! THAT IS JEROBOAM, MY CHIEF LABOR FOREMAN.

WHEN HER CURIOSITY IS SATISFIED, THE QUEEN OF SHEBA PRESENTS SOLOMON WITH GIFTS OF GOLD, RARE SPICES, PRECIOUS STONES — AND DEPARTS FOR HER HOME.

SOLOMON CONTINUES TO BUILD -- BU[T] NOW THE PEOPLE ARE WORRIED AN[D] SHOCKED BY WHAT THEY SEE.

ANOTHER TEMPLE TO THE IDOL OF ONE OF THE KING'S FOREIGN WIVES. AND OUR TAXES USED TO BUILD IT!

THOSE HEATHEN TEMPLES MAKE IT CLEAR THAT SOLOMON IS NO LONGER ASKING GOD FOR GUIDANCE. THERE'S TROUBLE AHEAD FOR ISRAEL...

...he King Is Dead

FROM 1 KINGS 11: 29—12: 3

THERE IS TROUBLE IN ISRAEL. HIGH TAXES ANGER THE PEOPLE... SOME EVEN TALK OF REVOLT. BUT KING SOLOMON REFUSES TO HEED THE WARNING SIGNS. ONE DAY AS THE KING'S LABOR FOREMAN, JEROBOAM, LEAVES JERUSALEM...

JEROBOAM! STOP! I HAVE A MESSAGE FOR YOU FROM GOD.

AHIJAH!

A MESSAGE FROM GOD? WHAT IS IT? AND WHY ARE YOU TEARING YOUR ROBE?

THIS IS HOW SOLOMON'S KINGDOM WILL BE TORN APART-- BECAUSE HE HAS TURNED AWAY FROM GOD.

AHIJAH TEARS THE ROBE INTO TWELVE STRIPS.

HERE, TAKE THESE TEN PIECES. THEY REPRESENT THE TEN TRIBES OF ISRAEL OVER WHICH YOU WILL RULE WHEN SOLOMON DIES. THE OTHER TWO TRIBES WILL BE GIVEN TO SOLOMON'S SON.

SOLOMON FLIES INTO A RAGE WHE HE LEARNS OF AHIJAH'S PROPHEC

I MADE JEROBOAM A LEADER-- NOW HE IS USING HIS POSITION TURN PEOPLE AGAINST ME! FIN HIM AND KILL HIM!

BUT FRIENDS WARN JEROBOAM-- AND HE ESCAPES INTO EGYPT.

I'LL STAY HERE UNTIL SOLOMON DIES. THEN WE'LL SEE IF AHIJAH SPOKE THE TRUTH ABOUT MY RULING THE NORTHERN TRIBES OF ISRAEL.

REPORTS OF YOUR PEOPLE'S COMPLAINTS HAVE BEEN REACHING US FOR SOME TIME.

BUT SOLOMON CONTINUES TO LIVE IN LUXURY--AND SO FAR REMOVED FROM HIS PEOPLE THAT THEIR COMPLAINTS DO NOT REACH HIM. HE EVEN IGNORES AHIJAH'S PROPHECY AND GOD'S WARNING THAT THE KINGDOM WILL BE DIVIDED BECAUSE HE WORSHIPS FALSE GODS.

AT LAST HE EVEN JOINS HIS FOREIGN WIVES IN THEIR WORSHIP OF HEATHEN IDOLS.

FIRST THE KING--AND NOW THE PEOPLE WORSHIP HEATHEN IDOLS. NO COUNTRY THAT TURNS AWAY FROM GOD CAN REMAIN STRONG AND FREE. ISRAEL IS DOOMED.

JUST TO PLEASE ME, PRAY TO MY GOD, SOLOMON.

IT CAN DO NO HARM--I STILL PRAY EVERY DAY TO THE GOD OF ISRAEL.

THEN SOLOMON DIES! WITH GOD'S HELP HE HAD BUILT ISRAEL INTO A STRONG NATION. BUT IN HIS GREED FOR MORE WEALTH AND POWER HE HAD TURNED AWAY FROM GOD--AND HIS MIGHTY KINGDOM BEGINS TO CRUMBLE...

WHILE ISRAEL MOURNS THE DEATH OF ITS KING, A MESSENGER CARRIES THE NEWS OF HIS DEATH TO EGYPT.

JEROBOAM, I BRING NEWS! KING SOLOMON IS DEAD. HIS SON, REHOBOAM, HAS TAKEN HIS PLACE. THE PEOPLE WANT YOU TO COME HOME AND PRESENT THEIR CASE TO THE NEW KING.

I'LL GO AT ONCE!

The Kingdom Is Divided

FROM 1 KINGS 12: 4-27

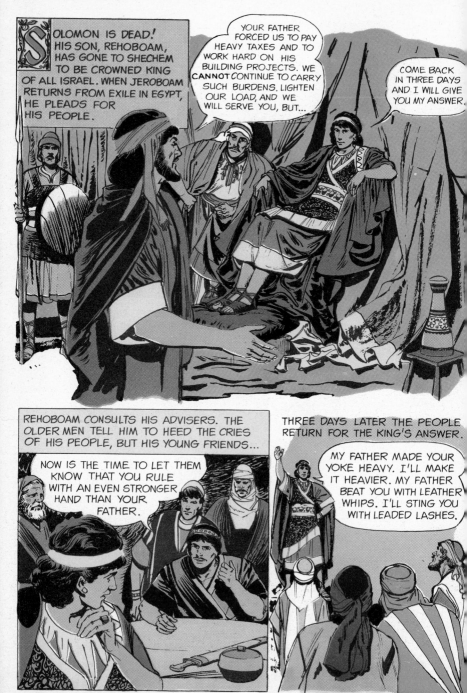

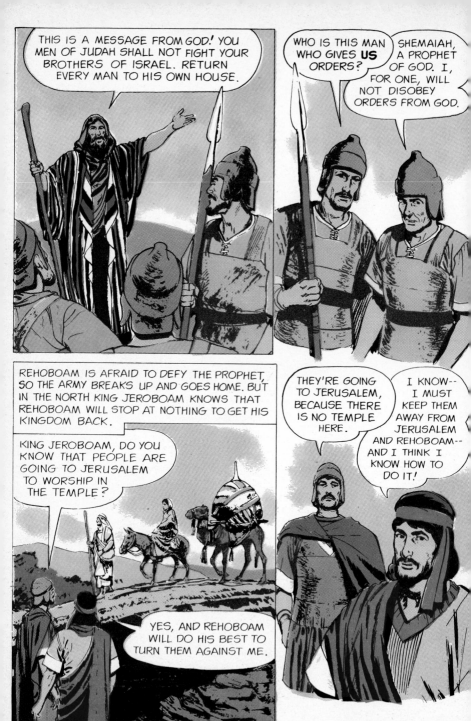

AHIJAH, THE PROPHET! HE TOLD ME I WOULD BE KING. HE KNOWS WHAT WILL HAPPEN. DISGUISE YOURSELF SO THAT HE WILL NOT KNOW YOU AND GO TO HIM.

IMMEDIATELY THE QUEEN DISGUISES HERSELF AND SETS OUT FOR AHIJAH'S HOUSE. BUT AS SHE STEPS THROUGH THE DOOR...

I AM BLIND-- BUT I KNOW WHO YOU ARE AND WHY YOU HAVE COME! TELL YOUR HUSBAND, JEROBOAM, THAT HE HAS DONE EVIL--AND EVIL WILL COME TO HIM! HIS CHILD WILL DIE -- AND ONE DAY THE PEOPLE OF ISRAEL WILL BE SCATTERED IN OTHER LANDS BECAUSE THEY HAVE WORSHIPED IDOL

THE FIRST PART OF AHIJAH'S PROPHECY COMES TRUE AT ONCE-- WHEN THE QUEEN RETURNS HOME SHE FINDS HER SON DEAD! BUT JEROBOAM IS NOT WISE ENOUGH TO HEED THIS WARNING. HE CONTINUES TO LEAD HIS PEOPLE IN IDOL WORSHIP, AND EVERY KING OF ISRAEL AFTER HIM FOLLOWS HIS EVIL PRACTICE. AT LAST KING AHAB COMES TO THE THRONE, AND...

ONE DAY A CARAVAN ENTERS SAMARIA, THE CAPITAL OF NORTHERN ISRAEL, WHERE KING AHAB HAS HIS PALACE.

THAT'S A RICH CARAVAN-- WONDER WHERE IT'S FROM AND WHO CAN AFFORD TO TRAVEL IN SUCH STYLE?

IT'S AHAB'S NEW WIFE-- JEZEBEL -- THE DAUGHTER OF THE HEATHEN KING OF TYRE.

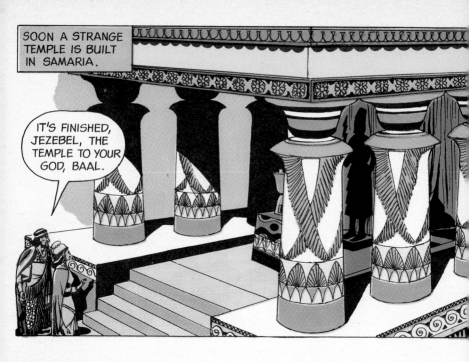

SOON A STRANGE TEMPLE IS BUILT IN SAMARIA.

IT'S FINISHED, JEZEBEL, THE TEMPLE TO YOUR GOD, BAAL.

MY GOD? YOUR GOD, AHAB, AND EVERYBODY'S GOD. ONLY BAAL SHALL BE WORSHIPED WHERE I AM QUEEN.

THAT WON'T BE EASY --THERE ARE STILL PEOPLE IN ISRAEL WHO WORSHIP ISRAEL'S GOD.

THEY'LL WORSHIP ISRAEL'S GOD NO LONGER-- I HAVE ORDERED THEM PUT TO DEATH!

A Prophet Speaks

FROM I KINGS 17: 1-7

AND AS SUDDENLY AS HE APPEARED, THE STRANGER IS GONE!

WHO WAS THAT MAN? WHO LET HIM IN? WHY DID YOU LET HIM GET AWAY?

THAT WAS ELIJAH — A PROPHET OF ISRAEL'S GOD. HE IS A MAN OF MYSTERY — HE COMES AND GOES LIKE THE WIND.

A PROPHET OF GOD? FIND HIM AND PUT HIM TO DEATH INSTANTLY.

WHAT DID THAT CRAZY MAN SAY ABOUT NO RAIN OR DEW UNTIL HE CALLS FOR IT? NONSENSE! BAAL CONTROLS THE RAIN.

ELIJAH IS A PROPHET OF GOD. I WONDER...

AND AS THE MONTHS GO BY, AHAB CONTINUES TO WONDER...

EVERYTHING IS DRYING FROM LACK OF RAIN. MAYBE ELIJAH DID HAVE SOMETHING TO DO WITH THIS DROUGHT.

PEOPLE OF ISRAEL! HOW LONG WILL YOU WANDER BACK AND FORTH BETWEEN THE LORD AND BAAL? IF BAAL IS GOD, WORSHIP HIM. IF THE LORD IS GOD, WORSHIP HIM AND HIM ONLY. BUT TODAY, YOU MUST CHOOSE.

LET ALL OF BAAL'S PROPHETS MAKE AN OFFERING AND PRAY TO HIM. I, ALONE, WILL PRAY TO THE LORD. THE GOD WHO ANSWERS WITH FIRE IS THE REAL GOD.

THAT'S A REAL TEST.

FAIR ENOUGH-- BUT IF ELIJAH FAILS, HE'LL LOSE HIS LIFE. AHAB WILL SEE TO THAT.

THE PROPHETS OF BAAL ARE FORCED TO ACCEPT THE CHALLENGE. WITH GREAT CEREMONY THEY PREPARE THE SACRIFICE... AND BEGIN TO CHANT AND CALL UPON THEIR GOD.

AS THE HOURS PASS THEY SING LOUDER AND LOUDER.

CALL A LITTLE LOUDER -- PERHAPS BAAL IS TALKING --OR OFF ON A JOURNEY-- OR ASLEEP.

BY MIDAFTERNOON THE PROPHETS ARE STILL CALLING UPON BAAL TO SEND DOWN FIRE-- BUT THERE IS NO ANSWER. AT LAST THEY GIVE UP.

THEN ELIJAH BUILDS AN ALTAR TO GOD.

WHEN IT IS FINISHED, AND THE SACRIFICE PREPARED, ELIJAH ORDERS MEN TO POU[R] WATER OVER IT.

POUR ON MO[RE] WATER, FILL T[HE] TRENCH WITH

THEN--BEFORE THE WATER-SOAKED ALTAR--ELIJAH PRAYS.

HEAR ME, O LORD, HEAR ME, THAT THE PEOPLE OF ISRAEL MAY KNOW THAT THOU ART THE LORD GOD.

IN THE HOMES OF ISRAEL, THERE IS JOY-- THANKSGIVING -- AND REPENTANCE.

RAIN AT LAST! THE LORD BE PRAISED!

YES, IT WAS THE LORD WHO ANSWERED WITH FIRE! WE SHOULD NEVER HAVE WORSHIPED BAAL.

BUT IN THE PALACE QUEEN JEZEBEL IS FURIOUS...

WHEN THE PEOPLE SAW THE FIRE FROM GOD, THEY TURNED ON THE PROPHETS OF BAAL AND KILLED THEM. ELIJAH---

ELIJAH! ELIJAH! THAT'S ALL I HEAR! WELL, I'LL HEAR HIS NAME NO MORE!

SHE CALLS FOR A MESSENGER.

GO TO ELIJAH AND TELL HIM THAT BY THIS TIME TOMORROW HE WILL BE AS THOSE PROPHETS HE HAD PUT TO DEATH ON MOUNT CARMEL...

A Voice in the Mountain

ROM 1 KINGS 19: 3-18

IN A FIT OF RAGE QUEEN JEZEBEL SENDS WORD TO ELIJAH THAT HE WILL BE PUT TO DEATH THE NEXT DAY. THAT NIGHT ELIJAH AND HIS SERVANT MAKE THEIR ESCAPE.

WHERE CAN WE GO TO BE SAFE?

THE DESERT-- EVEN JEZEBEL WON'T LOOK FOR US THERE.

THEIR JOURNEY TAKES THEM SOUTH THROUGH ISRAEL AND JUDAH. THE SERVANT STAYS IN THE CITY OF BEER-SHEBA, WHILE ELIJAH CONTINUES ALONE INTO THE WILDERNESS. BUT AFTER A DAY'S TRAVEL...

O LORD, TAKE MY LIFE. I HAVE DONE MY BEST TO BRING ISRAEL BACK TO THEE, BUT IT'S NO USE. THE PEOPLE WON'T LISTEN!

THEN, HUNGRY AND TIRED, ELIJAH FALLS ASLEEP. WHILE HE IS SLEEPING AN ANGEL APPEARS WITH BREAD AND WATER.

WAKE UP, ELIJAH, AND EAT.

ELIJAH IS ENCOURAGED BY THE FACT THAT GOD IS TAKING CARE OF HIM. AFTER HE EATS AND RESTS, HE CONTINUES HIS JOURNEY...

AND FORTY DAYS LATER HE REACHES MOUNT SINAI WHERE GOD TALKED TO MOSES.

I PRAY THAT I, TOO, MAY RECEIVE A MESSAGE FROM GOD ON THIS MOUNTAIN.

SUDDENLY A GREAT STORM STRIKES. THE WIND HURLS ROCKS DOWN THE MOUNTAIN-- AN EARTHQUAKE SHAKES THE GROUND ON WHICH ELIJAH STANDS -- AND LIGHTNING SPLITS THE SKY! THE POWER OF GOD IS REVEALED IN THE STORM -- BUT THERE IS NO MESSAGE.

THEN, IN THE QUIETNESS AFTER THE STORM, ELIJAH HEARS THE STILL, SMALL VOICE OF GOD.

ELIJAH, WHAT ARE YOU DOING HERE?

O LORD, THE PEOPLE OF ISRAEL DO NOT SERVE THEE. THEY WORSHIP IDOLS. THEY HAVE KILLED ALL OF YOUR OTHER PROPHETS--AND NOW THEY WANT TO KILL ME.

BUT GOD TELLS ELIJAH THERE IS WORK FOR HIM TO DO IN ISRAEL. SO--HIS COURAGE RENEWED-- ELIJAH STARTS BACK.

O GOD, I AM READY NOW TO FACE ANY DANGER.

Forged Letters

FROM 1 KINGS 19:19-21; 21:1-8

ELIJAH RETURNS TO ISRAEL TO SERVE AS GOD'S PROPHET. PASSING BY A FIELD HE STOPS AND THROWS HIS CLOAK OVER A YOUNG FARMER'S SHOULDERS.

ELIJAH! YOUR CLOAK! DOES THIS MEAN THAT YOU ARE CALLING **ME** TO BE A PROPHET?

YES, ELISHA, YOU HAVE BEEN APPOINTED BY GOD TO BE HIS SPOKESMAN IN ISRAEL.

WAIT--LET ME GO HOME AND SAY GOOD-BYE TO MY MOTHER AND FATHER; THEN I'LL GO WITH YOU.

OF COURSE--BUT JOIN ME SOON, FOR THERE IS WORK TO BE DONE FOR GOD.

SO ELISHA RETURNS HOME AND GIVES A FAREWELL FEAST FOR HIS FAMILY AND FRIENDS.

YOU'RE GIVING UP A SAFE LIFE FOR A DANGEROUS ONE, ELISHA.

I KNOW, BUT GOD HAS CALLED ME, AND I MUST OBEY.

I'M PROUD OF YOU, SON.

ELISHA GOES TO WORK WITH ELIJAH, AND WHILE THEY ARE TRAINING OTHER PROPHETS, KING AHAB MAKES A SURPRISE VISIT TO ONE OF HIS SUBJECTS.

NABOTH, I WANT TO BUY THIS VINEYARD. OR, IF YOU LIKE, I'LL GIVE YOU ANOTHER FOR IT.

I'M SORRY, O KING, BUT OUR FAMILY HAS OWNED THIS VINEYARD FOR MANY YEARS. IT WOULD NOT BE RIGHT TO SELL IT TO SOMEONE OUTSIDE THE FAMILY.

YOU MAY ALSO FIND THAT IT IS NOT RIGHT TO DISPLEASE YOUR KING!

LIKE A SPOILED CHILD WHO CANNOT HAVE HIS OWN WAY, AHAB RETURNS TO THE PALACE.

WHAT IS THE MATTER? ARE YOU ILL?

NO--I WANT NABOTH VINEYARD, BUT HE WON'T SELL IT TO ME

WON'T? ARE YOU KING OF ISRAEL, OR AREN'T YOU?

BUT DON'T WORRY, I'LL GET THE VINEYARD FOR YOU.

QUICKLY JEZEBEL WRITES SOME LETTERS AND SIGNS THE KING'S NAME TO THEM.

DELIVER THESE TO THE ELDERS AND NOBLES OF THE CITY.

AHAB IS SO FRIGHTENED BY ELIJAH'S PROPHECY THAT FOR A TIME HE SEEKS GOD'S FAVOR. BUT WHEN THE KING OF JUDAH COMES TO VISIT HIM, HE PREPARES FOR WAR IN SPITE OF GOD'S WARNING.

THE SYRIANS TOOK ONE OF MY CITIES. WILL YOU HELP ME DRIVE THEM OUT?

YOUR WAR IS MY WAR, AHAB.

THE ARMIES ARE FORMED, AND THE TWO KINGS LEAD THEIR FORCES ACROSS THE JORDAN RIVER TOWARD THE CONQUERED CITY. BUT AT THE THOUGHT OF THE COMING BATTLE, AHAB BECOMES FRIGHTENED.

I'LL DISGUISE MYSELF SO THE ENEMY WON'T RECOGNIZE ME!

The Last Journey

FROM II Kings 22: 30—II Kings 2: 10

AS KING AHAB OF ISRAEL PREPARES FOR BATTLE AGAINST THE SYRIAN INVADERS, HE BECOMES SO FRIGHTENED THAT HE DISGUISES HIMSELF.

THE ENEMY WILL NEVER RECOGNIZE ME IN THIS ARMOR.

AHAB IS RIGHT— THE ENEMY DOESN'T RECOGNIZE HIM. BUT IN THE HEAT OF BATTLE A STRAY ARROW STRIKES AHAB. ALTHOUGH BADLY WOUNDED, HE STAYS WITH HIS ARMY UNTIL EVENING.

THE BATTLE TURNS AGAINST THE ISRAELITES. SUDDENLY...

LOOK! THE KING IS DEAD!

WITHOUT THEIR KING, THE ISRAELITES RETREAT, AND THE CAMPAIGN FAILS. KING AHAB'S BODY IS BROUGHT BACK TO HIS CAPITAL FOR BURIAL, AND HIS CHARIOT TAKEN OUTSIDE THE CITY TO BE WASHED.

REMEMBER--ELIJAH SAID THAT AHAB'S FAMILY WOULD PAY FOR NABOTH'S MURDER.

YES, AND HE SAID THAT AHAB'S FAMILY WOULD BE DESTROYED. I WONDER IF THAT WILL COME TRU TOO.

AHAB'S KINGDOM PASSES ON TO HIS SONS, BUT QUEEN JEZEBEL REMAINS THE POWER BEHIND THE THRONE. IT IS DURING THE REIGN OF HER SECOND SON, JEHORAM, THAT ELIJAH RECEIVES A MESSAGE FROM GOD.

THE LORD HAS TOLD ME TO GO TO JORDAN. YOU DON'T NEED TO GO ALONG, ELISHA.

I WANT TO GO WITH YO ELIJAH.

Chariot of Fire!

FROM II Kings 2: 11-18; 4: 1

ELISHA ASKS FOR THE SPIRITUAL POWER TO CARRY ON ELIJAH'S WORK. AND ELIJAH PROMISES: "IF YOU SEE ME WHEN I AM TAKEN FROM YOU, IT WILL BE A SIGN THAT GOD HAS GRANTED YOUR WISH." SUDDENLY A CHARIOT OF FIRE SWEEPS DOWN AND SEPARATES ELIJAH FROM ELISHA, AND ELIJAH IS TAKEN UP IN A WHIRLWIND...

ELIJAH! ELIJAH! I SEE NOW--THE POWER THAT PROTECTED AND GUIDED YOU IS GREATER THAN ALL THE ARMIES OF EARTH!

FOR A LONG TIME ELISHA STANDS LOOKING UP INTO THE SKY. THEN, PICKING UP THE PROPHET'S CLOAK, HE TURNS BACK. AT THE JORDAN HE STRIKES THE WATER WITH HIS CLOAK--AND THE WATERS PART.

O GOD, I THANK THEE FOR THE GIFT OF THY POWER.

HERE IS THE MONEY I OWE YOU. NOW LET GO OF MY SON.

MONEY? I DON'T UNDERSTAND. I'LL --I'LL TAKE IT, BUT--

GOD SAVED US FROM SLAVERY, DIDN'T HE, MOTHER?

YES, THROUGH HIS PROPHET, ELISHA, WHO IS NEVER TOO BUSY TO HELP THOSE OF US WHO NEED HIM.

ELISHA HELPS MANY PEOPLE BY KEEPING THEIR FAITH IN GOD STRONG. STORIES OF HIS GOOD DEEDS SPREAD THROUGHOUT ALL OF ISRAEL.

EVEN TO A SMALL GIRL WHO WANDERS AWAY FROM HER FATHER'S FLOCK...

SHE'D MAKE A GOOD SLAVE FOR GENERAL NAAMAN'S WIFE.

YES--I'LL TAKE HER. THE REST OF YOU TAKE THE SHEEP.

A Prophet's Prescription

FROM II Kings 5: 1-14a

NAAMAN'S WIFE BELIEVES THE GIRL AND RUNS TO TELL HER HUSBAND. NAAMAN QUICKLY TAKES THE NEWS TO THE KING.

I CAN'T BELIEVE IT, NAAMAN, BUT I'LL GIVE YOU A LETTER TO TAKE TO THE KING OF ISRAEL.

IN SAMARIA, THE CAPITAL OF ISRAEL, NAAMAN HAS THE LETTER DELIVERED TO KING JEHORAM. THE LETTER DOES NOT MENTION ELISHA, SO THE KING MISINTERPRETS IT.

WHAT'S THIS— THE KING OF SYRIA ASKS **ME** TO CURE HIS GENERAL?

AM I A GOD THAT I CAN CURE AN INCURABLE DISEASE? IS THE KING OF SAMARIA TRYING TO PICK A QUARREL WITH ME?

REPORTS OF KING JEHORAM'S PROBLEM SPREAD THROUGHOUT THE CITY. WHEN ELISHA HEARS THEM HE SENDS HIS SERVANT TO THE KING.

ELISHA SAYS IF YOU SEND NAAMAN TO HIM, THE GENERAL WILL LEARN THE POWER OF GOD'S PROPHET.

I'LL SEND WORD TO NAAMAN AT ONCE.

NAAMAN LOSES NO TIME IN GOING TO ELISHA'S HOUSE WHERE HE IS MET BY A SERVANT.

GREETINGS, NAAMAN. ELISHA SAYS THAT IF YOU WILL WASH SEVEN TIMES IN THE JORDAN RIVER YOU WILL BE CURED.

WASH IN THE JORDAN? THAT'S SILLY! I THOUGHT ELISHA WOULD CALL ON HIS GOD TO CURE ME.

NAAMAN THINKS HE HAS BEEN MADE A FOOL OF -- AND IN A RAGE HE DRIVES AWAY.

THINK AGAIN, NAAMAN. IF ELISHA HAD ASKED YOU TO DO SOMETHING HARD, YOU WOULD HAVE DONE IT. WHY NOT DO THIS EASY THING HE ASKS?

THE GENERAL TAKES HIS SERVANT'S ADVICE AND GOES TO THE JORDAN RIVER.

I DON'T SEE HOW THIS MUDDY WATER WILL CURE LEPROSY.

Surrounded

FROM II Kings 5: 14-16; 6: 8-16

NAAMAN, A GENERAL OF THE SYRIAN ARMY, HAS LEPROSY. AT ELISHA'S DIRECTION, HE DIPS SEVEN TIMES IN THE JORDAN RIVER...

NAAMAN! LOOK-- YOUR SKIN IS AS CLEAR AS MINE!

I'M CURED! I'M CURED! I'M NO LONGER A LEPER!

OVERCOME WITH GRATITUDE, NAAMAN RETURNS AT ONCE TO ELISHA'S HOUSE...

NOW I KNOW THERE IS NO GOD EXCEPT ISRAEL'S GOD. PLEASE ACCEPT THESE GIFTS IN PAYMENT FOR WHAT YOU HAVE DONE FOR ME.

THANK YOU, NAAMAN, BUT I CAN ACCEPT NOTHING. IT WAS GOD-- NOT I-- WHO HEALED YOU.

I THANK GOD EVERY DAY FOR HEALING ME, AND I OWE IT ALL TO ELISHA...

AND TO THE LITTLE GIRL WHO ALSO BELIEVES IN ELISHA'S GOD.

BUT THE HEALING OF NAAMAN DOES NOT KEEP THE KING OF SYRIA FROM PLOTTING AGAINST ISRAEL.

MY SPIES TELL ME THAT THE KING OF ISRAEL WILL SOON BE RETURNING TO SAMARIA. SET UP AN AMBUSH AND CAPTURE HIM.

A FEW DAYS LATER ON THE ROAD TO SAMARIA...

STOP! ELISHA SENDS WORD FOR YOU TO TAKE ANOTHER ROAD. THE SYRIANS ARE WAITING ON THIS ROAD TO CAPTURE YOU.

FOR DAYS THE SYRIAN SOLDIERS WAIT FOR THE ISRAELITE KING -- BUT HE DOESN'T COME. AGAIN THE SYRIAN KING SETS A TRAP AND AGAIN ELISHA WARNS HIS KING TO ESCAPE. FINALLY THE SYRIAN KING BECOMES SO ANGRY THAT HE ACCUSES HIS OWN MEN OF TREASON.

WE'RE NOT GUILTY, O KING. IT'S ELISHA, THE PROPHET IN ISRAEL, WHO IS TELLING YOUR PLANS.

ELISHA, IS IT? HAVE OUR SPIES FIND OUT WHERE HE IS AND I'LL SEND AN ARMY TO GET HIM.

A FEW DAYS LATER...

I HAVE GOOD NEWS FOR YOU -- ELISHA IS AT DOTHAN.

SEND AN ARMY AT ONCE TO SURROUND THE CITY.

THE SYRIANS MARCH -- AND SET UP THEIR CAMP BY NIGHT. THE NEXT MORNING -- ELISHA'S SERVANT RISES EARLY AND SEES THE SYRIAN ARMY.

ELISHA! WE'RE SURROUNDED -- BY THE WHOLE SYRIAN ARMY!

FEAR NOT -- THERE'S MORE POWER ON OUR SIDE THAN ON THEIRS.

One Against an Army

FROM II Kings 6: 17-24

ELISHA'S SERVANT IS FRIGHTENED WHEN HE SEES THE SYRIAN ARMY. BUT AS ELISHA PRAYS, THE SERVANT LOOKS UP TO SEE CHARIOTS OF FIRE SURROUNDING THE PROPHET.

THE ARMY OF HEAVEN IS WITH ELISHA!

TO SAVE THE CITY FROM ATTACK, ELISHA AND HIS SERVANT GO OUT TO MEET THE ENEMY. AT ONCE THE SYRIAN SOLDIERS CLOSE IN ON THEM. BUT ELISHA PRAYS, AND SUDDENLY...

I CAN'T SEE -- WHAT'S HAPPENED?

I'M BLIND -- I --

COME WITH ME. I KNOW THE ONE YOU SEEK, AND I'LL TAKE YOU TO HIM.

ELISHA LEADS THE ENEMY SOLDIERS TEN MILES SOUTH AND INTO THE CAPITAL CITY OF ISRAEL.

O LORD, OPEN THEIR EYES, THAT THEY MAY SEE.

INSTANTLY, SIGHT RETURNS TO THE SYRIANS.

WE'RE IN SAMARIA--

WE'RE TRAPPED-- THEY'LL KILL US!

SHALL WE KILL THEM, ELISHA?

NO. FEED THEM AND SEND THEM HOME.

A Starving City

THIS IS THE MOMENT THE QUEEN MOTHER, JEZEBEL, HAS BEEN WAITING FOR.

YOUR PEOPLE ARE STARVING-- AND WHAT IS ELISHA'S GOD DOING ABOUT IT? NOTHING! GET RID OF ELISHA AND CALL ON MY GOD, BAAL!

YOU'RE RIGHT, MOTHER. I'LL ORDER HIM PUT TO DEATH AT ONCE.

AS KING JEHORAM'S SOLDIER SETS OUT ON HIS ERRAND OF DEATH, ELISHA IS VISITING WITH FRIENDS.

BAR THE DOOR, PLEASE. THE KING IS SENDING A SOLDIER TO KILL ME.

HOW COULD ELISHA KNOW THAT?

BUT THE KING SUDDENLY BECOMES WORRIED ABOUT KILLING THE PROPHET. HE RUSHES AFTER HIS SOLDIER, AND REACHES ELISHA JUST IN TIME.

IF GOD ISN'T GOING TO HELP US, WE MIGHT AS WELL SURRENDER NOW. OUR PEOPLE ARE STARVING.

NO! THE LORD SAYS THERE WILL BE FOOD ENOUGH FOR EVERYONE TOMORROW.

THE ANXIOUS KING IS WILLING TO WAIT UNTIL THE NEXT DAY, BUT OUTSIDE THE CITY FOUR LEPERS HAVE NOT HEARD ELISHA'S PROPHECY...

I'M STARVING. I'M GOING TO TRY TO BREAK INTO THE CITY AND GET SOME FOOD.

WHY DO THAT? THERE'S NO FOOD IN THERE.

THEN LET'S GO OVER TO THE SYRIAN CAMP. MAYBE THEY'LL GIVE US SOMETHING TO EAT. MAYBE THEY'LL KILL US. EITHER WAY, THERE'S NOTHING TO LOSE-- WE'LL STARVE IF WE STAY HERE.

IN DESPERATION THE FOUR HUNGRY LEPERS APPROACH THE SYRIAN CAMP.

SOMETHING STRANGE IS GOING ON. THERE'S NOT A GUARD IN SIGHT. MAYBE IT'S A TRAP--

MAYBE IT IS-- BUT I'D RATHER DIE QUICKLY THAN STARVE TO DEATH. COME ON--

THERE'S NOBODY HERE!

The Missing Enemy

THEIR HUNGER SATISFIED, THE LEPERS QUICKLY SEARCH THE SYRIAN TENTS.

MORE GOLD-- WE'RE RICH!

LOOK! WON'T PEOPLE BE SURPRISED TO SEE ME IN THIS?

SURPRISED? THEY'LL SAY YOU STOLE IT. THEN YOU'LL REALLY BE IN TROUBLE.

HE'S RIGHT-- LET'S HIDE EVERYTHING.

ISN'T RIGHT FOR US TO KEEP ALL OF THIS FOOD FROM THE STARVING PEOPLE IN THE CITY.

IF WE DON'T TELL THE GOOD NEWS, SOME PUNISHMENT MAY COME UPON US.

THE MEN GO BACK TO THE CITY AND POUND ON THE GATES UNTIL A GUARD ANSWERS.

THE SYRIANS ARE GONE!

GONE? WHERE? HOW DO YOU KNOW?

The Sound of Marching Men

FROM II KINGS 7: 14—9: 12

WE RODE AROUND YOUR CAMP. THERE WAS NO SIGN OF EVEN A SCOUTING PARTY-- LET ALONE **TWO** ARMIES. DID YOU REALLY **SEE** THEM?

NO--BUT WE HEARD THEM! THOUSANDS OF SOLDIERS, HORSES AND CHARIOTS --WE WOULDN'T HAVE HAD A CHANCE AGAINST SUCH MIGHT.

THE **SOUND** OF ARMIES-- REAL ENOUGH TO FRIGHTEN THE WHOLE SYRIAN CAMP. WHAT DO YOU MAKE OF IT?

IT WAS A MIRACLE--USED BY ELISHA'S GOD TO FRIGHTEN THE SYRIANS AWAY.

ELISHA'S GOD--YES. THAT FITS IN WITH THE PROMISE THAT BY TODAY THERE WOULD BE FOOD FOR EVERYONE!

BACK IN SAMARIA THE STARVING ISRAELITES RUSH OUT TO THE SYRIAN CAMP, EAT THEIR FILL, AND HAUL THE REST OF THE FOOD BACK TO THE CITY.

YOU SAID THERE WOULD BE FOOD, ELISHA, BUT I DIDN'T BELIEVE YOU.

IT WAS THE LORD WHO PROMISED THE FOOD--AND YOU CAN ALWAYS COUNT ON THE PROMISES OF GOD!

WHEN THE NEWS REACHES KING JEHORAM, HE BELIEVES JEHU IS BRINGING NEWS OF THE WAR. SO, WITH HIS VISITOR, KING AHAZIAH OF JUDAH, HE RIDES OUT TO MEET JEHU.

DO YOU BRING NEWS OF PEACE?

HOW CAN THERE BE PEACE IN ISRAEL WHILE YOUR MOTHER, JEZEBEL, WORSHIPS BAAL?

TOO LATE, JEHORAM SEES THAT JEHU HAS COME TO OVERTHROW THE KINGDOM. HE TRIES TO ESCAPE, BUT JEHU'S ARROW STRIKES HIM DOWN.

THAT'S THE FIRST BLOW STRUCK FOR ISRAEL.

BUT NOT THE LAST! NOW JEZEBEL MUST PAY FOR HER SINS!

IN SPITE OF JEHU'S SURPRISE ATTACK, THE NEWS REACHES THE PALACE BEFORE HE DOES...

QUEEN JEZEBEL! JEHU HAS KILLED YOUR SON-- HIS MEN ARE AFTER THE KING OF JUDAH. JEHU--

JEHU! HE'LL BE HERE NEXT.

QUICKLY SHE PUTS ON HER CROWN-- AND GOES TO THE WINDOW IN TIME TO SEE JEHU RIDE THROUGH THE GATE

THERE SHE IS-- JEZEBEL, THE MOST EVIL WOMAN IN ALL ISRAEL!

WHO IS ON MY SIDE?

TO THE SOUTH, IN THE KINGDOM OF JUDAH, JEZEBEL'S DAUGHTER, ATHALIAH, RECEIVES THE NEWS...

I BRING BAD NEWS. YOUR MOTHER, QUEEN JEZEBEL, AND YOUR SON, KING AHAZIAH, HAVE BEEN KILLED BY ISRAEL'S NEW KING--JEHU.

POOR LITTLE JOASH! YOUR FATHER IS DEAD, AND YOUR GRANDMOTHER HATES YOU.

STOP WHISPERING. TAKE MY GRANDSON AWAY AND LEAVE ME ALONE IN MY TERRIBLE GRIEF.

BUT ATHALIAH'S GRIEF IS ONLY A COVER FOR HER PLAN.

MY SON IS DEAD. NOW IF **HIS** SONS WERE DEAD, **I** COULD RULE OVER JUDAH. THEN WE WOULD BE FREE TO WORSHIP BAAL.

SHE ACTS AT ONCE TO CARRY OUT HER BOLD PLOT.

ORDER YOUR SOLDIERS TO KILL ALL OF THE KING'S MALE RELATIVES. DON'T LET ONE OF THEM ESCAPE--NOT ONE!

The Temple Secret

FROM II Kings 11: 1-12

UNDER COVER OF DARKNESS THE TWO WOMEN HURRY TO THE TEMPLE OF GOD. THE HIGH PRIEST, JEHOIADA, ANSWERS THEIR FRANTIC KNOCK.

WE HAVE BABY JOASH. HELP US SAVE HIM FROM THE QUEEN.

COME IN-- HURRY!

ONLY THE PRIESTS USE THIS ROOM. JOASH WILL BE SAFE HERE AS LONG AS IT IS NECESSARY TO HIDE HIM.

FEW HOURS LATER THE QUEEN'S OFFICER GIVES HIS REPORT.

THE KING'S RELATIVES HAVE BEEN PUT TO DEATH AS YOU COMMANDED.

GOOD!

NOW THERE IS NO ONE TO SAY I CANNOT RULE JUDAH.

FOR SIX YEARS ATHALIAH RULES JUDAH WITH A CRUEL HAND UNTIL AT LAST THE PEOPLE BEGIN TO COMPLAIN. UNKNOWN TO THEM -- IN A SECRET ROOM OF THE TEMPLE -- YOUNG PRINCE JOASH IS BEING TRAINED BY THE HIGH PRIEST.

WHAT'S THIS?

THE IDOL BAAL -- THE CAUSE OF ALL THE TROUBLE IN JUDAH. YOUR GRANDMOTHER WORSHIPS IT. WHEN YOU ARE KING, YOU MUST DESTROY IT AND LEAD YOUR PEOPLE BACK TO GOD.

NOW, TELL ME THE WORD OF GOD YOU HAVE LEARNED TODAY.

THOU SHALT LOVE THE LORD THY GOD WITH ALL THINE HEART, AND WITH ALL THY SOUL, AND WITH ALL THY MIGHT!

WHO IS HE?

YOUR GRANDSON, JOASH, NOW KING OF JUDAH.

THAT'S A LIE— JOASH IS DEA[D] GET RID OF THIS BOY!

STOP! TAKE HER OUT OF THE TEMPLE!

QUEEN ATHALIAH IS FORCED FROM THE TEMPLE, AND PUT TO DEATH.

IN THE TEMPLE THE CORONATION OF KING JOASH CONTINUES...

DO YOU PROMISE TO OBEY GOD'S LAW AND RULE YOUR PEOPLE ACCORDING TO HIS WORD?

I PROMISE!

UNDER THE GUIDANCE OF JEHOIADA, THE HIGH PRIEST, JOASH DESTROYS THE TEMPLE OF BAAL AND LEADS HIS PEOPLE BACK TO THE WORSHIP OF GOD. THE HOUSE OF GOD IS REPAIRED, AND FOR YEARS JUDAH PROSPERS. BUT WHEN JEHOIADA DIES, JOASH IS TOO WEAK TO STAND UP UNDER THE PRESSURE OF THOSE WHO WOULD TURN HIM AWAY FROM GOD. FINALLY, JEHOIADA'S SON, ZECHARIAH, GOES TO THE KING...

KING JOASH, I SPEAK TO YOU AS MY FATHER WOULD SPEAK. YOUR PEOPLE ARE RETURNING TO BAAL AND FORSAKING GOD. JUDAH WILL BE DESTROYED UNLESS YOU STOP THEM!

AS SOON AS ZECHARIAH LEAVES, THE WORSHIPERS OF BAAL GIVE **THEIR** ADVICE.

ZECHARIAH IS A TROUBLE-MAKER.

HE SHOULD BE PUT TO DEATH BEFORE HE TURNS ALL JUDAH AGAINST YOU.

YOU'RE RIGHT. STIR UP THE PEOPLE SO THAT THEY WILL GET RID OF HIM.

AND SO JOASH, WHO WAS ONCE A GOOD KING, LISTENS TO EVIL ADVICE. ZECHARIAH IS STONED TO DEATH BY A MOB--AND SOON HIS PROPHECY OF DISASTER COMES TRUE...

Dagger in the Night

FROM II KINGS 12—18: 10

WHEN KING JOASH TURNED AWAY FROM GOD, ZECHARIAH PREDICTED DISASTER. IT COMES SOON-- IN AN ATTACK BY THE KING OF SYRIA WHO IS ON A CAMPAIGN OF CONQUEST. DURING THE ATTACK THE MEN WHO HAD ADVISED JOASH AGAINST ZECHARIAH ARE KILLED. IN AN ATTEMPT TO SAVE JERUSALEM, JOASH TRIES TO BUY OFF THE ENEMY.

GIFTS FROM MY LORD, KING JOASH OF JUDAH. HE ASKS THAT YOU ACCEPT THEM AND LEAVE JERUSALEM IN PEACE.

TELL YOUR KING I ACCEPT HIS OFFER.

HAVING ACQUIRED AN EASY FORTUNE, THE KING OF SYRIA CALLS BACK HIS ARMY AND MARCHES ON. JERUSALEM IS SAVED, BUT JOASH FALLS GRAVELY ILL.

HOW IS THE KING TODAY?

NO BETTER-- NO WORSE. TOO BAD THE SYRIANS DIDN'T KILL THE KING ALONG WITH THE MEN WHO ADVISED HIM TO MURDER ZECHARIAH. WITH THEM GONE WE COULD SAVE JUDAH --IF IT WEREN'T FOR...

IF YOU'RE THINKING WHAT I AM--

SH! THIS ISN'T THE TIME.

BUT THAT NIGHT-- WHEN ALL THE PALACE IS ASLEEP...

REMEMBER-- WE'RE DOING THIS TO SAVE OUR COUNTRY.

SO KING JOASH IS MURDERED-- BY HIS OWN MEN. FOR ALMOST A HUNDRED YEARS JUDAH IS RULED BY KINGS WHO WAVER BETWEEN WORSHIPING GOD AND HEATHEN IDOLS. THEN HEZEKIAH COMES TO THE THRONE...

THEN HEZEKIAH CALLS THE PEOPLE TOGETHER...

DO NOT BE AFRAID. THERE IS MORE POWER ON OUR SIDE THAN ON THE SIDE OF THE ENEMY. THE LORD GOD IS WITH US.

BUT INSTEAD OF MAKING AN ARMED ATTACK ON THE CITY, THE ASSYRIAN KING SENDS A TASK FORCE TO TRY TO FRIGHTEN THE PEOPLE OF JERUSALEM INTO SURRENDERING.

WE HAVE CONQUERED OTHER CITIES AND COUNTRIES. WHAT MAKES YOU THINK YOUR GOD CAN SAVE YOU?

AFTER A WHILE THIS KIND OF ATTACK BEGINS TO HAVE ITS EFFECT.

HOW DO WE KNOW GOD WILL SAVE US?

OTHER CITIES HAVE FALLEN. AND, REMEMBER IT WAS THE ASSYRIANS WHO TOOK ISRAEL.

A Foolish King

FROM II CHRONICLES 32: 21—33: 12

WHEN THE ASSYRIANS SUDDENLY STOP THREATENING THE PEOPLE OF JERUSALEM, KING HEZEKIAH SENDS MEN TO SCOUT THE ENEMY CAMP. THEY FIND IT STRANGELY QUIET.

WHY-- THEY'RE ASLEEP, OR--

A PLAGUE MUST HAVE STRUCK DOWN THE MAIN FORCE OF THE ENEMY.

AT THE NEWS, ALL JERUSALEM GOES WILD WITH JOY...

HEZEKIAH SAID GOD WAS ON OUR SIDE.

AND GOD DOESN'T FORSAKE THOSE WHO BELIEVE AND TRUST HIM...

NO SOONER IS MANASSEH ON THE THRONE THAN THE FOLLOWERS OF BAAL BEGIN THEIR CAMPAIGN TO LEAD HIM AWAY FROM GOD.

TO BECOME RICH AND POWERFUL AS THE ASSYRIANS, WE SHOULD WORSHIP IDOLS, AS THEY DO.

NEVER AGAIN WHILE HEZEKIAH LIVES DO THE ASSYRIANS TRY TO TAKE JERUSALEM. HEZEKIAH CONTINUES TO LEAD HIS PEOPLE IN THEIR WORSHIP OF GOD, AND THEY ARE HAPPY. AT HIS DEATH, HIS YOUNG SON, MANASSEH, IS CROWNED KING.

MANASSEH LISTENS TO THEIR ADVICE, AND RESTORES IDOL WORSHIP IN ISRAEL. HE EVEN DARES TO PLACE AN IDOL IN THE TEMPLE OF GOD.

BUT WORSHIPING THE IDOLS OF THE SURROUNDING NATIONS DOES NOT SAVE MANASSEH. THE ASSYRIAN KING SUSPECTS MANASSEH IS PLOTTING AGAINST HIM AND SENDS TROOPS TO JERUSALEM. IN A SURPRISE MOVE THE ASSYRIANS OVERCOME MANASSEH'S FORCES AND TAKE THE KING PRISONER.

NO ONE KNOWS WHAT PROMPTED THE ASSYRIAN KING TO FREE MANASSEH--BUT WHEN HE RE-TURNS TO JERUSALEM HIS PEOPLE WELCOME HIM...

THE KING HAS RETURNED!

LONG LIVE THE KING OF JUDAH!

BUT THE PEOPLE ARE AMAZED AT HIS FIRST SPEECH...

I WAS WRONG TO TURN AWAY FROM GOD. DESTROY THE IDOLS, AND JOIN ME IN WORSHIPING GOD.

MANASSEH TRIES TO SAVE HIS NATION, BUT IT IS TOO LATE. MOST OF THE PEOPLE CONTINUE TO WORSHIP IDOLS. MANASSEH DIES, AND AFTER TWO YEARS, HIS EIGHT-YEAR-OLD GRANDSON, JOSIAH, COMES TO THE THRONE.

AS THE KING GROWS UP, THE IDOL WORSHIPERS TRY TO INFLUENCE JOSIAH, BUT THE YOUNG KING REMAINS TRUE TO GOD. HE RULES JUDAH WITH A FIRM BUT JUST HAND. ONE DAY HE CALLS FOR THREE OF HIS OFFICIALS.

THE WALLS OF THE TEMPLE ARE CRUMBLING-- I WANT THEM REPAIRED IMMEDIATELY.

WORKMEN BEGIN AT ONCE. AFTER A WHILE THE HIGH PRIEST COMES TO CHECK THEIR PROGRESS...

STOP! WHAT'S THAT OBJECT BEHIND THOSE STONES?

HE TAKES HIS DISCOVERY TO THE KING'S SCRIBE.

LOOK WHAT I HAVE FOUND! THE BOOK OF THE LAW!

IT HAS BEEN LOST FOR YEARS! LET ME READ IT!

SLOWLY, CAREFULLY, THE SCRIBE READS THE ANCIENT SCROLL.

WHAT DOES IT SAY?

IT GIVES GOD'S LAWS--BUT IT ALSO TELLS WHAT WILL HAPPEN IF THE LAWS ARE NOT OBEYED. I MUST READ THIS TO THE KING.

BUT I'M AFRAID THERE'S NOTHING HE--OR ANYBODY ELSE--CAN DO TO SAVE JUDAH!

A Prophetess Speaks

FROM II KINGS 22:11—24:20; II CHRONICLES 34:19—36:16.

THE SCRIBE READS TO KING JOSIAH FROM THE LOST BOOK THAT HAS BEEN FOUND IN THE TEMPLE WALLS.

GOD'S LAWS ARE CLEARLY STATED --AND SO IS THE PUNISHMENT FOR ANYONE WHO DISOBEYS THEM.

THEN JUDAH IS DOOMED! FOR IT HAS BROKEN GOD'S LAW MANY TIMES.

JOSIAH IS SO UPSET THAT HE QUICKLY SENDS SEVERAL HIGH-RANKING OFFICIALS TO THE PROPHETESS HULDAH.

THE KING HAS SENT US TO ASK FOR A MESSAGE FROM GOD ABOUT THE BOOK WE HAVE JUST READ.

THUS SAITH THE LORD: BECAUSE JUDAH HAS DISOBEYED ME, JUDAH SHALL BE DESTROYED... BUT THE DESTRUCTION WILL NOT COME IN THE DAYS OF JOSIAH.

HOPING HE MAY YET WIN GOD'S FORGIVENESS FOR HIS NATION, JOSIAH CALLS A MEETING OF THE PEOPLE.

AT JOSIAH'S COMMAND PAGAN WORSHIP IS WIPED OUT IN ALL THE LAND. OBJECTS USED IN IDOL WORSHIP ARE REMOVED FROM GOD'S TEMPLE IN JERUSALEM, TAKEN OUTSIDE THE CITY, AND BURNED.

I HAVE READ GOD'S LAWS TO YOU. LET US NOW PROMISE TO OBEY THEM FROM THIS DAY ON. AND MAY GOD HAVE MERCY ON US.

THEN JOSIAH CALLS THE PEOPLE TO KEEP THE FEAST OF THE PASSOVER.

THIS REMINDS US OF HOW GOD DELIVERED OUR FORE-FATHERS FROM SLAVERY IN EGYPT CENTURIES AGO.

WHILE JOSIAH LIVES, JUDAH OBEYS THE LAWS OF GOD. BUT AFTER HIS DEATH, ONE KING AFTER ANOTHER TURNS BACK TO THE WORSHIP OF IDOLS. LACKING GOD'S HELP, JUDAH COMES UNDER THE CONTROL OF A NEW WORLD POWER, BABYLONIA.

JUDAH IS ALLOWED TO REMAIN UNDER ITS OWN RULERS, BUT AFTER KING ZEDEKIAH COMES TO THE THRONE HE FOOLISHLY TRIES TO REGAIN HIS COUNTRY'S INDEPENDENCE. IN REPLY THE GREAT BABYLONIAN ARMY SETS OUT...

he Fall of Jerusalem

OM II CHRONICLES 36: 17-20; II KINGS 25: 1-11

FOR 2 YEARS AND A HALF, FORCES FROM THE GREAT BABYLONIAN ARMY BESIEGE THE CITY OF JERUSALEM. AT LAST THEY BREAK THROUGH THE WALL...

THAT NIGHT KING ZEDEKIAH AND HIS ARMY TRY TO ESCAPE.

IF WE CAN MAKE IT TO THE HILL REGION EAST OF THE JORDAN, THEY'LL NEVER FIND US.

IT'S OUR ONLY CHANCE --IF THEY CAPTURE US...

BUT THE BABYLONIANS PURSUE THEM, AND ZEDEKIAH IS CAPTURED BEFORE HE CAN REACH THE RIVER. HE IS BLINDED AND TAKEN TO BABYLON.

HUNGRY, WEARY, AND AFRAID, THE PEOPLE OF JERUSALEM ARE FORCED TO BEGIN THE LONG MARCH OF 900 MILES FROM JERUSALEM TO BABYLON--AS CAPTIVES.

GOD HAS FORSAKEN US.

NO. GOD WARNED US, BUT WE WOULD NOT LISTEN. IT IS WE WHO HAVE FORSAKEN GOD!

Return of the Captives

FROM EZRA 1, 2

FROM THE MOMENT THEY ARE CARRIED AWAY AS CAPTIVES TO BABYLON, THE JEWS DREAM OF RETURNING TO THEIR HOMELAND, JUDAH. THE BOOK OF **EZRA** TELLS WHAT HAPPENS TO THAT DREAM.

FOR MANY YEARS THE JEW LIVE AS CAPTIVES OF THE GREAT BABYLONIAN EMPIRE THEY WATCH ANXIOUSLY AS PERSIA, A STRONG COUNTR' TO THE EAST, RISES UP TO CHALLENGE BABYLON.

WHEN THE PERSIAN ARMY APPEARS OUTSIDE THE CITY WALLS, KING BELSHAZZAR IS SO SURE OF BABYLON'S STRENGTH THAT HE SPENDS THE NIGHT IN A DRUNKEN FEAST WITH HIS COURT. PERSIAN TROOPS STEAL INTO THE CITY-- INVADE THE PALACE--AND SLAY BELSHAZZAR. WITHIN HOURS THE BABYLONIAN EMPIRE FALLS TO PERSIA.

TWO WEEKS LATER KING CYRUS OF PERSIA RIDES TRIUMPHANTLY INTO THE CITY.

SO THAT'S OUR NEW RULER. I WONDER--DOES THIS MEAN GOOD OR EVIL FOR US JEWS?

I'VE HEARD THAT CYRUS IS A JUST MAN. WE'LL HAVE TO WAIT AND SEE.

SOON AFTER CYRUS TAKES OVER THE BABYLONIAN EMPIRE, AN OFFICIAL ANNOUNCEMENT IS READ.

THESE ARE THE WORDS OF KING CYRUS: THE GOD OF ISRAEL COMMANDS THAT A HOUSE BE BUILT FOR HIM IN JERUSALEM. ANY OF HIS PEOPLE WHO WANT TO DO SO MAY RETURN. THOSE WHO DO NOT GO BACK SHOULD GIVE OF THEIR POSSESSIONS TO HELP THOSE WHO RETURN TO JUDAH.

GIFTS OF MONEY, HORSES, MULES, CAMELS, GOLD AND SILVER, FOOD AND CLOTHING POUR IN. AT LAST THE DAY COMES WHEN THE GREAT CARAVAN IS READY TO LEAVE.

THANK GOD, I'LL SEE MY HOMELAND AGAIN.

ON THE LONG ROAD HOME, THEY FOLLOW MUCH THE SAME ROUTE THAT ABRAHAM, THE FATHER OF THE JEWISH NATION, TRAVELED 1,500 YEARS BEFORE WHEN HE OBEYED GOD'S COMMAND TO LEAVE UR AND MAKE A NEW NATION IN PALESTINE.

WHEN WE LEFT JERUSALEM IT WAS IN FLAMES -- I WONDER WHAT IT LOOKS LIKE NOW.

BUT NO MATTER HOW MUCH THEY PREPARE THEMSELVES FOR THE RUINED CITY, THEY ARE BROKENHEARTED WHEN THEY WALK THROUGH THE RUBBLE OF JERUSALEM.

SOLOMON'S BEAUTIFUL TEMPLE STOOD OVER THERE.

OUR HOME-- LET'S TRY TO FIND IT.

HOW PROUD WE WERE WHEN WE BUILT IT-- WITH OUR OWN HANDS, TOO. NOW LOOK AT IT-- A HOME FOR WILD DOGS.

MAYBE WE SHOULD NOT HAVE COME BACK. MAYBE...

OUR FOREFATHERS BUILT MUCH OF THIS CITY. WE'LL REBUILD IT -- JERUSALEM WILL RISE AGAIN. YOU'LL SEE...

A City Rises Again

BUT THE SOUND OF REJOICING BRINGS TROUBLE. THE SAMARITANS WHO LIVE NEAR JERUSALEM COME WITH A REQUEST TO HELP BUILD THE TEMPLE.

WE'RE SORRY-- BUT YOU DO NOT WORSHIP AS WE DO, SO WE CANNOT LET YOU HELP US BUILD OUR TEMPLE TO GOD.

SO THEY "CAN'T" LET US HELP THEM BUILD THE TEMPLE! WELL, WE'LL MAKE THEM SORRY THEY EVER CAME BACK TO JERUSALEM TO BUILD ANYTHING.

WHAT DO YOU MEAN?

THE JEWS SOON LEARN WHAT THE SAMARITAN MEANT. ONE DAY WHILE THEY ARE AT WORK AN OFFICER OF KING CYRUS RIDES UP.

BY ORDER OF THE KING, THIS WORK IS TO STOP!

STOP? WHY? IT WAS KING CYRUS HIMSELF WHO TOLD US WE SHOULD RETURN TO JERUSALEM TO REBUILD THE TEMPLE!

UNHAPPILY, THE WORKMEN LAY DOWN THEIR TOOLS AND GO HOME.

FATHER, WHAT COULD HAVE HAPPENED? KING CYRUS SAID...

YES, BUT THE SAMARITANS WROTE HIM THAT WE WERE TRYING TO DESTROY HIS POWER HERE. THE KING IS INVESTIGATING THE CHARGES AND HAS ORDERED WORK ON THE TEMPLE STOPPED.

FORCED TO OBEY, THE JEWS TURN TO WORK ON THEIR HOMES AND GARDENS. SEVERAL YEARS PASS -- CYRUS DIES AND NEW KINGS COME TO THE THRONE IN PERSIA, BUT STILL THE TEMPLE IN JERUSALEM IS NOT COMPLETED. THEN, ONE DAY, THE JEWS ARE APPROACHED BY TWO PROPHETS OF GOD.

HAGGAI, ZECHARIAH! WHAT BRINGS YOU HERE?

WE HAVE NEWS.

A NEW KING, DARIUS, HAS COME TO THE THRONE. LET'S START WORK AGAIN ON THE TEMPLE -- MAYBE HE WON'T STOP US.

KING DARIUS NOT ONLY LETS THE JEWS COMPLETE THE TEMPLE -- HE EVEN ORDERS HIS OFFICERS TO GIVE THEM THE MATERIAL THEY NEED.

SO -- AT LAST -- THE NEW TEMPLE OF GOD IS FINISHED. WITH THANKFUL HEARTS THE PEOPLE OFFER THEIR SACRIFICES AND PRAYERS TO GOD.

SOME YEARS LATER, EZRA, A PRIEST, GAINS PERMISSION FROM THE PERSIAN KING TO GO TO JERUSALEM TO TEACH THE PEOPLE THE LAWS OF GOD. HE TAKES A GROUP OF JEWS WITH HIM. UNDER EZRA JERUSALEM GROWS IN SIZE AND SPIRITUAL STRENGTH, BUT IS STILL WITHOUT WALLS AND SURROUNDED BY HOSTILE NEIGHBORS.

ONE NIGHT, WHILE THE CITY SLEEPS, A STRANGER AND HIS GUARDS RIDE TOWARD JERUSALEM ...

Two Lines of Defense

FROM NEHEMIAH

THE NEXT DAY NEHEMIAH CALLS ON THE PRIESTS AND RULERS OF THE CITY.

I HAVE EXAMINED THE WALLS OF JERUSALEM. THEY ARE JUST HEAPS OF BROKEN STONE. THE CITY IS DEFENSELESS.

YOU ARE RIGHT, BUT WHY--

WHY HAVE I COME? BECAUSE I, TOO, AM A JEW. AND WHILE I WAS SERVING THE KING OF PERSIA AS HIS CUPBEARER, I LEARNED THAT JERUSALEM WAS WITHOUT ANY DEFENSE. I PRAYED TO GOD-- AND THE KING GAVE ME HIS PERMISSION TO COME HERE AND BUILD UP THE WALLS. ARE YOU WITH ME?

WE ARE-- AND WE'LL START AT ONCE.

THE WORK BEGINS. EVERY ABLE-BODIED MAN AND BOY DOES HIS PART. THE WOMEN HELP... AND SLOWLY THE WALLS BEGIN TO RISE.

BUT SOME OF THE NEIGHBORING COUNTRIES DO NOT WANT TO SEE JERUSALEM PROTECTED.

IF THOSE WALLS ARE FINISHED, THE CITY WILL BE TOO STRONG TO ATTACK. WE MUST STOP IT **NOW**.

DOWN WITH THE WALLS!

BUT WHILE THE ENEMIES OF JERUSALEM PLAN TO TAKE THE CITY, NEHEMIAH PREPARES TO DEFEND IT.

PASS THESE OUT TO EVERY WORKER. LET NO MAN WORK WITHOUT A WEAPON IN HIS HAND -- READY TO FIGHT!

THE ENEMY APPROACHES -- BUT TO THEIR SURPRISE ARMED WORKERS RISE UP -- THEIR SPEARS RAISED AND THEIR BOWS PULLED.

THEY'RE ARMED!

RETREAT!

THE WORKERS GO BACK TO THEIR JOBS, AND SOON STRONG WALLS AND HEAVY GATES AGAIN PROTECT THE CITY OF JERUSALEM. BUT INSIDE THERE IS AN EVEN STRONGER LINE OF DEFENSE -- A NATION LED BY EZRA AND NEHEMIAH TO LOVE AND OBEY GOD!

THE BOOK OF ESTHER IS THE STORY OF A YOUNG JEWISH WOMAN WHO RISKS HER LIFE TO SAVE HER PEOPLE.

WHEN THE BABYLONIANS CAPTURE JERUSALEM, THEY TAKE THOUSANDS OF JEWS BACK HOME AS CAPTIVES. LATER, WHEN THE PERSIAN KING CONQUERS BABYLON, HE FREES THE JEWS. MANY RETURN TO JERUSALEM, BUT OTHERS REMAIN IN BABYLON AND PERSIA.

AT THIS TIME THE PERSIAN EMPIRE IS THE MOST POWERFUL IN ALL THE WORLD--REACHING FROM INDIA TO ETHIOPIA. ON THE THRONE AT SHUSHAN SITS KING AHASUERUS.

FOR MONTHS THE KING HAS BEEN ENTERTAINING HIGH-RANKING OFFICIALS OF HIS REALM. HOW MUCH LONGER WILL THIS FEASTING GO ON?

UNTIL HE HAS IMPRESSED ALL OF HIS SUBJECTS WITH HIS WEALTH AND POWER.

Plot Against the King

FROM ESTHER 2:11—3:6

FOR MONTHS, ESTHER, ALONG WITH HUNDREDS OF BEAUTIFUL WOMEN OF PERSIA, LIVES IN THE PALACE, WAITING FOR THE KING TO CHOOSE ONE OF THEM TO BE HIS WIFE. AT LAST THE KING MAKES HIS CHOICE --

ESTHER, YOU ARE NOW MY WIFE, QUEEN OF ALL PERSIA!

I AM HONORED, MY LORD.

BUT ESTHER'S COUSIN, MORDECAI, IS NOT INVITED TO THE WEDDING. HE SITS, AS HE DOES EVERY DAY, AT THE PALACE GATE, WAITING FOR A CHANCE WORD ABOUT ESTHER.

THE QUEEN OF PERSIA IS A JEWESS. BUT ONLY ESTHER AND I KNOW THAT!

HAMAN IS VERY PROUD AND ENJOYS HAVING PEOPLE BOW BEFORE HIM. BUT MORDECAI REFUSES TO RISE FROM HIS PLACE BY THE GATE.

WHO IS THAT MAN WHO DOES NOT SHOW PROPER RESPECT FOR ME?

THAT'S MORDECAI — A JEW. AND JEWS BOW ONLY TO THEIR GOD.

MORDECAI WILL PAY FOR THIS -- AND SO WILL EVERY JEW IN PERSIA!

Revenge!

THE ORDERS ARE WRITTEN AND DELIVERED. THROUGHOUT THE KINGDOM JEWISH FAMILIES ARE TERRIFIED...

WHY? WHY? WE HAVE DONE NO WRONG!

AND WHEREVER WE GO THERE'S A PRICE ON OUR HEADS!

WHEN MORDECAI HEARS THE ORDER HE DRESSES IN CLOTHES OF MOURNING AND POURS ASHES OVER HIS HEAD TO SHOW HIS GRIEF...

FROM HER PALACE WINDOW ESTHER SEES THAT SOMETHING IS WRONG.

FIND OUT WHAT IS TROUBLING MORDECAI.

THE QUEEN ASKS WHY I MOURN? DOESN'T SHE KNOW THAT HAMAN'S ORDER MEANS DEATH TO EVERY JEW IN PERSIA? SHOW THIS TO HER-- TELL HER SHE MUST GO TO THE KING AND ASK HIM TO SPARE THE JEWS.

A Queen Risks Her Life

FROM ESTHER 5:1—6:10

QUEEN ESTHER BREAKS A LAW BY APPEARING UNINVITED BEFORE THE KING--AN ACT PUNISHABLE BY DEATH. BUT THE LIVES OF HER PEOPLE, THE JEWS, ARE IN DANGER, AND SHE IS THE ONLY ONE WHO MAY BE ABLE TO SAVE THEM.

ESTHER! WHAT DOES SH[E] WANT THAT SH[E] WOULD RISK HE[R] LIFE TO GET[?]

SURPRISED AS HE IS BY HER SUDDEN APPEARANCE, THE KING IS PLEASED AT THE SIGHT OF HIS BEAUTIFUL QUEEN. HE HOLDS OUT HIS SCEPTER TO SHOW THAT SHE IS FORGIVEN, AND ASKS WHAT SHE WANTS.

I ASK THAT YOU AND HAMAN COME TO A DINNER THAT I SHALL PREPARE FOR YOU.

THE KING ACCEPTS. SO DOES HAMAN WHO IS OVERJOYED UNTIL HE LEAVES THE PALACE.

THAT STUBBORN JEW -- HE STILL WON'T BOW BEFORE ME! WELL, HE'LL SOON BE DEAD WITH ALL THE OTHER JEWS.

AT HOME HAMAN COMPLAINS THAT MORDECAI HAS INSULTED HIM.

DON'T STAND FOR IT, HAMAN. BUILD A GALLOWS AND TELL THE KING YOU WANT MORDECAI HANGED. THEN YOU CAN ENJOY YOUR DINNER WITH THE QUEEN.

I'LL DO IT! I'LL HAVE THE GAL- LOWS MADE AND GO TO SEE THE KING EARLY IN THE MORNING.

BUT THAT NIGHT THE KING CANNOT SLEEP. HE CALLS FOR A SCRIBE TO READ TO HIM FROM THE RECORDS OF THE KINGDOM. WHEN THE READING REACHES THE STORY OF MORDECAI, THE KING INTERRUPTS.

STOP! WHAT REWARD DID HE RECEIVE FOR SAVING MY LIFE?

NONE, MY LORD.

AT THAT MOMENT HAMAN ENTE THE COURT AND IS BROUGH BEFORE THE KING.

HAMAN, YOU'RE JUST THE MAN I WANTED TO SEE. WHAT SHALL I DO TO HONOR A MA WHO HAS PLEASED ME?

I KNEW THE KING WOULD RECOGNIZE MY SERVICES.

LET HIM WEAR ONE OF YOUR ROBES -- AND RIDE YOUR HORSE. THEN HAVE ONE OF YOUR NOBLES LEAD HIM THROUGH THE CITY TELLING EVERYONE THAT THIS IS THE WAY THE KING HONORS THOSE WHO PLEASE HIM.

GOOD! GET THE ROBE AND THE HORSE AND DO EXACTLY AS YOU HAVE SUGGESTED -- FOR MORDECAI.

MORDECAI! BUT I -- YES -- SIR!

The Unchangeable Law

FROM ESTHER 6: 11—10

WHAT IS IT? I'LL GRANT WHATEVER YOU ASK.

I ASK FOR THE LIFE OF MYSELF AND MY PEOPLE. BY THE CRUEL PLAN OF A CERTAIN MAN WE ARE TO BE PUT TO DEATH.

PUT **YOU** TO DEATH? WHO WOULD DARE DO SUCH A THING?

HAMAN!

N OW, FOR THE FIRST TIME THE KING KNOWS THAT HIS WIFE IS JEWISH, AND THAT HAMAN TRICKED HIM INTO SIGNING HER DEATH WARRANT. IN ANGER THE KING LEAVES THE ROOM.

QUEEN ESTHER! I'LL DO ANYTHING YOU SAY-- ONLY SPARE ME! SPARE ME!

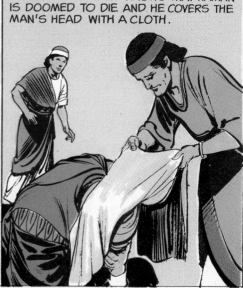

THE KING'S SERVANT KNOWS THAT HAMAN IS DOOMED TO DIE AND HE COVERS THE MAN'S HEAD WITH A CLOTH.

HAMAN BUILT A GALLOWS ON WHICH HE WANTED TO HANG MORDECAI.

AND ON THAT GALLOWS HAMAN SHALL HANG. TAKE HIM AWAY.

YOU SHALL HAVE HAMAN'S WEALTH FOR THE SUFFERING HE HAS CAUSED YOU.

MY COUSIN, MORDECAI, HAS SUFFERED, TOO.

MORDECAI IS YOUR COUSIN? I'LL PUT HIM IN HAMAN'S PLACE -- SECOND IN POWER IN ALL OF MY KINGDOM. WITH HAMAN OUT OF THE WAY, NO ONE WILL DARE TO HARM EITHER OF YOU.

A FEW DAYS LATER ESTHER TAKES THE SECOND STEP IN HER CAMPAIGN.

IF I HAVE PLEASED YOU, I BEG YOU TO TAKE BACK THE ORDER HAMAN SENT TO KILL ALL THE JEWS.

I WISH I COULD. BUT ACCORDING TO PERSIAN LAW, NO MAN -- NOT EVEN I -- CAN CANCEL AN ORDER THAT HAS BEEN SIGNED WITH MY SEAL.

BUT--I CAN SEND A NEW ORDER!

THE ORDER IS WRITTEN AND RUSHED TO GOVERNORS THROUGHOUT THE EMPIRE.

LISTEN--THE KING SAYS THE JEWS MAY ARM TO PROTECT THEMSELVES, AND THAT MORDECAI, A JEW, HAS BEEN MADE PRIME MINISTER.

AH! THE KING IS ON THE SIDE OF THE JEWS! WE'D BETTER BE, TOO.

ON THE THIRTEENTH DAY OF THE 12TH MONTH THE JEWS THROUGHOUT THE PERSIAN EMPIRE GATHER TOGETHER TO DEFEND THEMSELVES. WITH THE HELP OF THE KING'S GOVERNORS, THEY ARE SUCCESSFUL.

AND AT THE PALACE...

I'VE WRITTEN AN ORDER THAT EVERY YEAR ALL JEWS MUST CELEBRATE THE DAYS WHEN WE WERE SAVED FROM OUR ENEMY. THEY SHOULD BE DAYS OF JOY AND GIVING OF GIFTS, AND SHALL BE CALLED THE FEAST OF PURIM.

THE FEAST OF PURIM IS STILL CELEBRATED BY JEWISH PEOPLE THROUGHOUT THE WORLD.

A Man with a Message

THINGS SEEMED TO BE GOING WELL IN THE LAND OF JUDAH, BUT TROUBLE WAS ON THE WAY. IN THEIR HEARTS THE PEOPLE WERE TURNING AWAY FROM GOD. THE RICH WERE CHEATING THE POOR. AND ALTHOUGH THE WALLS OF JERUSALEM WERE STRONG, THERE WAS ALWAYS THE DANGER OF INVASION BY AN ENEMY. IN THIS TIME OF NEED, GOD SENT A YOUNG MAN WITH A MESSAGE. HE WAS ISAIAH, ONE OF THE GREATEST OF THE HEBREW PROPHETS.

HOLY, HOLY, HOLY, IS THE LORD GOD OF HOSTS.

THE CALL TO BECOME A PROPHET OF GOD COMES TO ISAIAH WHEN HE IS WORSHIPING IN THE TEMPLE. AS HE PRAYS, HE SEES A GLORIOUS VISION.

O GOD, I AM NOT WORTHY TO BE IN THY PRESENCE. I AM A SINFUL MAN IN A SINFUL NATION.

AN ANGEL TOUCHES ISAIAH'S LIPS WITH A COAL OF FIRE AND SAYS, "YOUR SIN IS TAKEN AWAY." THEN ISAIAH HEARS GOD ASK: "WHOM SHALL I SEND TO SPEAK TO THIS SINFUL NATION?"

HERE I AM; SEND ME.

A Call from God

FROM JEREMIAH 1; II KINGS 22: 1—23: 29

"JUDAH WILL BE DESTROYED FOR DISOBEYING GOD!" THE PROPHET ISAIAH WARNED. BUT THE PEOPLE OF JUDAH IGNORED THE WARNING AND CONTINUED THEIR MAD RUSH TOWARDS RUIN. THEN GOD CALLED ANOTHER PROPHET NAMED JEREMIAH TO SOUND THE ALARM AGAIN.

IT'S AN EXCITING DAY FOR JEREMIAH WHEN HE GOES TO JERUSALEM WITH HIS FATHER TO SEE JUDAH'S NEW KING.

LONG LIVE KING JOSIAH!

WHY! HE'S JUST ABOUT MY AGE! I WONDER WHAT IT WOULD BE LIKE TO HAVE SUCH AN IMPORTANT JOB.

A FEW YEARS LATER JEREMIAH FINDS OUT, FOR GOD CALLS HIM TO AN EVEN GREATER TASK-- TO BECOME SPOKESMAN FOR HIM.

O GOD-- I DON'T KNOW HOW TO SPEAK SO THAT PEOPLE WILL LISTEN. I'M TOO YOUNG FOR SUCH A BIG JOB.

E SOON FINDS OUT-- WHEN HE TELLS THE PRIESTS
HIS OWN TOWN THAT JUDAH WILL BE DESTROYED
ECAUSE THE PEOPLE HAVE TURNED FROM GOD
O WORSHIP IDOLS.

WHO IS THIS YOUNG UPSTART TO TELL US HOW TO LIVE?

LET'S GET RID OF HIM BEFORE HE STARTS TROUBLE.

SO, TO SAVE HIS LIFE, JEREMIAH IS FORCED TO LEAVE HIS HOME TOWN AND GO TO JERUSALEM.

KING JOSIAH LOVES AND WORSHIPS GOD; HE WILL HELP ME TRY TO SAVE JUDAH.

OR SEVERAL YEARS JEREMIAH AND THE KING
ORK TOGETHER TO DESTROY IDOL WORSHIP. THEN,
NE DAY, JEREMIAH HEARS SOME FRIGHTENING NEWS.

HE ASSYRIAN EMPIRE
CRACKING UP. EGYPT
MARCHING NORTH TO
RAB WHAT'S LEFT. KING
OSIAH DECLARES HE
ILL STOP THE EGYPTIAN
RMY FROM MARCHING
THROUGH JUDAH.

STOP EGYPT? WHY, IT'S ONE OF THE STRONGEST COUNTRIES IN THE WORLD! THE KING IS MAKING A BIG MISTAKE.

MEDITERRANEAN

EGYPT

JUDAH

ASSYRIAN EMPIRE

BUT KING JOSIAH LEADS HIS SOLDIERS OUT OF THE GATES OF JERUSALEM —AND INTO THE PATH OF THE ONCOMING EGYPTIAN ARMY.

The Broken Vase

FROM JEREMIAH 18—20: 2; II KINGS 23: 30-37

KING JOSIAH IS KILLED AS HE ATTEMPTS TO DEFEAT THE EGYPTIANS. NOW HIS SON, JEHOIAKIM, SITS ON THE THRONE OF JUDAH AS A PUPPET RULER FOR EGYPT. AT ONCE THE IDOL WORSHIPERS BEGIN THEIR CAMPAIGN AGAINST GOD AND HIS PROPHET, JEREMIAH.

O KING, YOUR FATHER ORDERED US NOT TO WORSHIP ANY GOD BUT JEHOVAH. AND WHAT HAPPENED? JUDAH IS NO LONGER A FREE COUNTRY. JOIN US IN WORSHIPING OUR GODS SO THAT JUDAH WILL BECOME STRONG-- LIKE OUR NEIGHBORS.

JEHOIAKIM AGREES--AND IN SPITE OF JEREMIAH'S WARNINGS, MANY OF THE PEOPLE FOLLOW THE KING'S LEAD.

GO AWAY, JEREMIAH. NOBODY WANTS TO LISTEN TO YOUR FAR-FETCHED STORIES ABOUT JUDAH BEING DESTROYED!

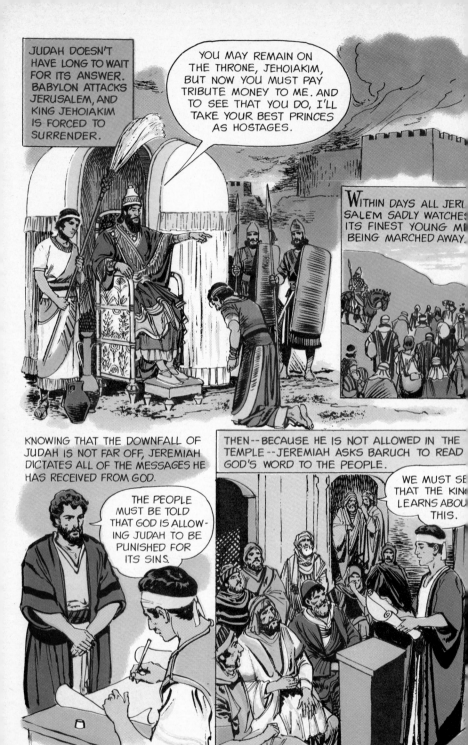

AS THE SCROLL IS READ TO THE KING, HE BECOMES SO ANGRY THAT HE CUTS IT UP PIECE BY PIECE AND THROWS IT INTO THE FIRE.

ARREST JEREMIAH AND BARUCH. THROW THEM INTO PRISON. THAT WILL KEEP THEM QUIET.

BUT JEREMIAH AND BARUCH ARE PREPARED FOR THE KING'S ANGER-- ALREADY THEY ARE IN HIDING.

THE KING BURNED THE SCROLL -- BUT WE WILL WRITE ANOTHER.

WHILE JEREMIAH AND BARUCH ARE BUSY REPLACING THE BURNED SCROLL, TROUBLE IS BREWING IN THE PALACE.

WHY SHOULD WE PAY TRIBUTE TO BABYLON? I SAY LET'S STOP IT AND USE THE MONEY TO BUILD UP OUR OWN ARMY. THEN WE'LL BE READY IF BABYLON ATTACKS US AGAIN.

YOU'RE RIGHT-- THOSE HOSTAGES IN BABYLON ARE NOT AS IMPORTANT AS ALL OF US HERE IN JUDAH.

IN TIME, WORD LEAKS OUT THAT KING JEHOIAKIM IS BREAKING HIS AGREEMENT WITH BABYLON. JEREMIAH IS ALARMED.

THE KING'S DECISION IS AGAINST THE WILL OF GOD. AND NO MAN CAN DEFY GOD!

Rebellion

FROM II KINGS 24: 1-6;
Jeremiah 27; 28: 1-12; 37: 1-10.

JUDAH MADE AN AGREEMENT WITH BABYLON, AND JUDAH WILL BE PUNISHED FOR BREAKING IT.

KING JEHOIAKIM'S REVOLT AGAINST BABYLON IS WELL UNDER WAY -- WHEN -- SUDDENLY -- HE DIES. HIS SON, JEHOIACHIN, COMES TO THE THRONE AND PLEDGES TO UPHOLD HIS FATHER'S STAND FOR JUDAH'S FREEDOM. IN SPITE OF THE KING'S OPPOSITION, JEREMIAH REPEATS HIS WARNING.

JEREMIAH KNOWS THAT THE TIME IS SHORT, BUT HE CONTINUES TO PLEAD WITH HIS PEOPLE TO STOP THE REVOLT. HIS PLEAS ARE IGNORED. THEN ONE DAY...

THE BABYLONIANS ARE COMING!

WITH FULL FORCE THE ARMY OF BABYLON STORMS THE WALLS OF JERUSALEM.

YOUNG KING JEHOIACHIN, WHO HAS RULED THREE MONTHS, IS FORCED TO SURRENDER TO KING NEBUCHADNEZZAR.

THIS TIME I WILL TAKE YOUR TREASURES, YOUR NOBLES, YOUR SKILLED WORKERS **AND** YOUR KING. LET THIS BE A LESSON TO YOU WHO ARE LEFT!

SO JEREMIAH'S PROPHECY COMES TRUE! THE TEMPLE TREASURES ARE LOOTED, THE KING AND 10,000 OF JUDAH'S ABLEST MEN ARE LED AWAY. PRINCE ZEDEKIAH IS MADE KING-- **AFTER** HE PROMISES LOYALTY TO BABYLON.

FOR A FEW YEARS KING ZEDEKIAH PAYS TRIBUTE TO BABYLON. THEN, IN SPITE OF JEREMIAH'S WARNINGS, HE BEGINS TO LISTEN TO SOME HOT-HEADED YOUNG ADVISERS IN HIS COURT.

WHAT DO **WE** GET FROM THE MONEY PAID TO BABYLON?

WELL-- WE GET PEACE.

PEACE--BUT NOT FREEDOM! MAYBE THE EGYPTIANS WILL HELP US-- THEY HATE BABYLON, TOO.

LET ME THINK ABOUT IT.

WHEN JEREMIAH LEARNS THAT THERE IS TALK OF ANOTHER REVOLT, HE PUTS AN OX YOKE ON HIS SHOULDERS AND WALKS THROUGH THE STREETS.

WHAT'S THE MEANING OF THIS?

BABYLON HAS STRUCK TWICE, AND IT WILL STRIKE AGAIN. THE NEXT TIME IT WILL DESTROY JERUSALEM. JUDAH'S ONLY HOPE OF SURVIVAL IS TO WEAR THE YOKE OF BABYLON AS I AM WEARING THIS ONE.

I'LL SHOW YOU WHAT TO DO WITH THE YOKE OF BABYLON. BREAK IT!

DURING ALL OF THIS TIME, EGYPT KEEPS AN ANXIOUS EYE ON THE GROWING TENSIONS IN JUDAH. AT THE RIGHT MOMENT IT SENDS AN AMBASSADOR TO KING ZEDEKIAH.

BABYLON IS YOUR ENEMY AS WELL AS OURS. ALONE, NEITHER ONE OF US CAN DEFEAT THEM, BUT--

TOGETHER WE CAN! AND WE WILL!

Accused

FROM JEREMIAH 37—38: 6.

THEN -- SUDDENLY -- THE ATTACK CEASES...

THE BABYLONIANS ARE BREAKING CAMP-- THEY'VE GIVEN UP THE SIEGE!

WE'VE WON! JUDAH IS FREE!

LONG LIVE KING ZEDEKIAH!

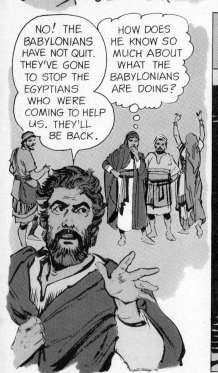

NO! THE BABYLONIANS HAVE NOT QUIT. THEY'VE GONE TO STOP THE EGYPTIANS WHO WERE COMING TO HELP US. THEY'LL BE BACK.

HOW DOES HE KNOW SO MUCH ABOUT WHAT THE BABYLONIANS ARE DOING?

A FEW DAYS LATER JEREMIAH STARTS ON A TRIP TO HIS HOME TOWN -- A FEW MILES FROM JERUSALEM. BUT BEFORE HE GETS OUT OF THE GATE, HE IS STOPPED.

HALT! YOU'RE UNDER ARREST!

WHY? I HAVE DONE NOTHING WRONG.

IN SPITE OF HIS INNOCENCE, JEREMIAH IS THROWN INTO PRISON. WITHIN A FEW WEEKS THE BABYLONIANS, AFTER DEFEATING THE EGYPTIANS, RETURN TO THE GATES OF JERUSALEM. JEREMIAH'S ENEMIES BRING HIM BEFORE THE KING AND ACCUSE HIM OF BEING A TRAITOR.

I REPEAT THE WARNING GOD HAS GIVEN ME. INVADERS FROM THE NORTH WILL CONQUER JUDAH. GOD HAS CHOSEN THE BABYLONIANS TO DESTROY OUR NATION BECAUSE OF THE SINS OF ITS PEOPLE.

IT'S THIS KIND OF TALK THAT MAKES OUR SOLDIERS LOSE COURAGE. PUT THIS TRAITOR TO DEATH--OR THE CITY **WILL** FALL.

HE IS IN YOUR HANDS--DO WHAT YOU WANT WITH HIM.

QUICKLY--BEFORE THE KING CAN CHANGE HIS MIND-- JEREMIAH IS PUT INTO AN OLD CISTERN BENEATH THE PRISON FLOOR.

LET HIM STARVE TO DEATH!

A Prophecy Comes True

FROM JEREMIAH 38: 7—43: 7.

JEREMIAH IS TAKEN BACK TO PRISON... THE SIEGE GOES ON, BUT AT THE END OF 30 MONTHS...

THE BABYLONIANS HAVE BROKEN THROUGH THE WALL!

JERUSALEM WILL BE DESTROYED! BUT IT WILL RISE AGAIN... AND SOMEDAY GOD'S COMMANDMENTS WILL BE WRITTEN IN THE HEARTS OF MEN WHO CHOOSE TO OBEY GOD. THEY WILL LIVE TOGETHER IN PEACE.

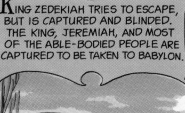

KING ZEDEKIAH TRIES TO ESCAPE, BUT IS CAPTURED AND BLINDED. THE KING, JEREMIAH, AND MOST OF THE ABLE-BODIED PEOPLE ARE CAPTURED TO BE TAKEN TO BABYLON.

BUT IN THE CAPTIVE CAMP AT RAMAH...

THE KING OF BABYLON HAS LEARNED THAT YOU TRIED TO KEEP YOUR COUNTRY FROM REBELLING AGAINST HIM, SO HE HAS SENT ORDERS TO SET YOU FREE.

THANK GOD! NOW I CAN HELP THE PEOPLE WHO HAVE BEEN LEFT IN ISRAEL WITHOUT A LEADER.

ABOUT A MONTH AFTER JERUSALEM IS TAKEN, A BABYLONIAN OFFICER RETURNS, TAKES MORE CAPTIVES, AND THEN SETS FIRE TO THE CITY.

THE FIRE RAGES FOR DAYS -- UNTIL THE ONCE-PROUD CAPITAL OF JUDAH BECOMES A HEAP OF SMOULDERING RUINS.

THE BABYLONIANS SET UP HEADQUARTERS AT MIZPAH AND APPOINT AN ISRAELITE TO ACT AS GOVERNOR. JEREMIAH JOINS HIM -- AND BECOMES HIS ADVISER.

TOGETHER WE'LL ENCOURAGE THE PEOPLE TO BUILD UP THEIR HOMES AND REPLANT THEIR VINEYARDS AND FIELDS.

SOMEDAY THE CAPTIVES WILL RETURN-- AND JUDAH WILL BECOME A NATION AGAIN.

BUT BEFORE THE GOVERNOR'S DREAM CAN COME TRUE HE IS MURDERED BY SOME ISRAELITES WHO ARE JEALOUS OF HIS POWER IN THE COUNTRY. FEARFUL THAT BABYLON WILL BLAME ALL ISRAEL FOR THE MURDER, A GROUP OF PEOPLE GO TO JEREMIAH...

WE WANT TO GO TO EGYPT-- WHERE THERE IS PEACE AND PLENTY TO EAT.

YOU WILL FIND NEITHER PEACE NOR PLENTY IN EGYPT. STAY HERE -- THE BABYLONIANS WILL NOT HURT YOU.

BUT THE PEOPLE DO NOT BELIEVE JEREMIAH. THEY FLEE TO EGYPT, FORCING HIM TO GO WITH THEM. AND THERE, UNTIL HE DIES, JEREMIAH TRIES TO LEAD HIS PEOPLE BACK TO GOD.

THE GRIEF OF THE JEWS OVER THE DESTRUCTION OF JERUSALEM IS EXPRESSED IN A GROUP OF POEMS FOUND IN THE

BOOK OF LAMENTATIONS

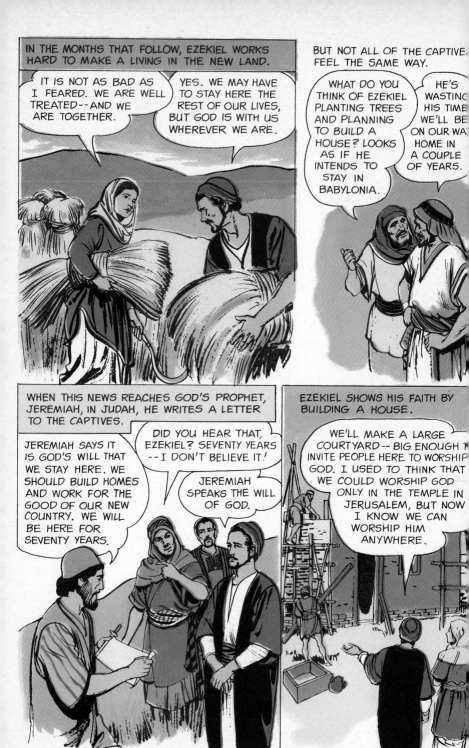

EZEKIEL KEEPS WARNING THE PEOPLE THAT JERUSALEM [WI]LL BE DESTROYED, [BU]T THEY REFUSE [TO] BELIEVE HIM. [TH]EN -- SUDDENLY-- [EZ]EKIEL'S WIFE [DI]ES. BUT THE [PR]OPHET SHOWS [NO] OUTWARD SIGN [OF] GRIEF.

WE MOURN FOR YOUR WIFE, EZEKIEL. WHY DO YOU NOT MOURN FOR THE ONE YOU LOVED?

YES, I LOVED HER VERY MUCH. BUT **GOD** HAS COMMANDED ME NOT TO SHOW MY GRIEF, AS A SIGN THAT YOU ARE NOT TO SHOW YOUR GRIEF WHEN JERUSALEM FALLS.

[B]UT THE PEOPLE WILL NOT GIVE UP BELIEVING THAT [J]ERUSALEM WILL BE STANDING--STRONG AND BEAUTIFUL-- [W]AITING FOR THEIR RETURN. ONE DAY A MAN [S]TAGGERS WEARILY INTO THEIR MIDST...

WHAT BRINGS YOU HERE?

I'M FROM WHAT **WAS** JERUSALEM.

YOU HAVE ALL PASSED -- NOW YOU'LL BE GIVEN THREE YEARS TO STUDY UNDER OUR WISE MEN. AFTER THAT THE KING HIMSELF WILL CHOOSE THOSE BEST QUALIFIED TO BE HIS ADVISERS.

O GOD, THANK YOU. HELP US TO PASS THESE NEW TESTS SO THAT WE MAY ADVISE THE KING IN A WAY THAT WILL PLEASE YOU.

THE YOUNG MEN ARE TAKEN AT ONCE TO THE PALACE TO BEGIN THEIR STUDIES. THEY ARE GIVEN THE BEST OF EVERYTHING -- EVEN FOOD FROM THE KING'S TABLE.

THANK YOU, BUT WE CANNOT EAT THIS MEAT AND DRINK THIS WINE. OUR HEBREW LAWS FORBID IT. GIVE US PLAIN FOOD AND WATER, PLEASE.

BUT IT'S THE KING'S ORDER -- WE DARE NOT DISOBEY. I LIKE YOU, DANIEL, BUT I DON'T WANT TO GET INTO TROUBLE.

GIVE US A TEN-DAY TRIAL. LET US EAT OUR FOOD AND THEN SEE IF WE ARE NOT STRONGER THAN THE OTHERS.

THE TEST IS MADE, AND AT THE END OF TEN DAYS, THERE'S NO DOUBT--DANIEL AND HIS FRIENDS NOT ONLY **LOOK** STRONGER, THEY **ARE** STRONGER.

AT THE END OF THREE YEARS, THE YOUNG MEN ARE BROUGHT BEFORE THE KING. HE TALKS WITH EACH ONE, THEN MAKES HIS DECISION.

I HAVE CHOSEN THESE FOUR--DANIEL, SHADRACH, MESHACH, AND ABEDNEGO -- TO SERVE AS MY ADVISERS.

THERE IS NONE TO EQUAL THEM, SIR.

The Statue

FROM DANIEL 2: 16-48

KING NEBUCHADNEZZAR IS FURIOUS! HIS WISE MEN CANNOT TELL HIM WHAT HE HAS DREAMED. SO HE ORDERS ALL OF THEM PUT TO DEATH-- INCLUDING DANIEL AND HIS THREE FRIENDS, SHADRACH, MESHACH, AND ABEDNEGO. DANIEL ASKS FOR PERMISSION TO SPEAK TO THE KING.

O KING, GIVE ME TIME AND I WILL TELL YOU WHAT YOU DREAMED.

YOU HAVE UNTIL TOMORROW AT THIS HOUR-- BUT NOT ONE MINUTE MORE.

DANIEL RUSHES BACK TO HIS FRIENDS WITH THE GOOD NEWS.

BUT, DANIEL, NO MAN ON EARTH CAN DO WHAT YOU HAVE PROMISED TO DO.

YOU ARE RIGHT-- NO MAN CAN DO IT, BUT GOD CAN. AND WE WILL ASK HIM TO GIVE US THE ANSWER.

DANIEL RELAYS THE GOOD NEWS TO HIS
HEBREW FRIENDS.

THE KING HAS MADE
ME RULER OVER BABYLON
AND EACH OF YOU HAS AN
IMPORTANT OFFICE IN
THE KINGDOM.

THAT'S
WONDERFUL!

BUT THE NEWS DOES NOT PLEASE
THE KING'S OTHER ADVISERS.

SO THE KING HAS PUT
THIS YOUNG HEBREW
OVER **US!** WE MUST
GET RID OF HIM.

NOT NOW—
HE'S TOO
POWERFUL.
BUT IF WE
CAN TURN THE
KING AGAINST
DANIEL'S FRIENDS
WE MIGHT BE ABLE
TO CAUSE DANIEL
TROUBLE.

THEIR OPPORTUNITY COMES WHEN THE KING
BUILDS A STATUE AND ORDERS HIS OFFICIALS
TO WORSHIP IT--OR BE THROWN INTO A FIERY
FURNACE.

THE KING IS PLAYING
RIGHT INTO OUR HANDS
--HE DOESN'T KNOW
THAT HEBREWS
WILL WORSHIP
ONLY THEIR GOD.

DANIEL HOLDS TOO
HIGH A POSITION
FOR ANY ONE OF
US TO REPORT ON
HIM-- BUT NOT
HIS FRIENDS...

RIGHT--AND TOMORROW
WHEN THE TRUMPET SOUNDS
FOR ALL MEN TO BOW BEFORE
THE STATUE, WE'LL KEEP OUR
EYES ON SHADRACH, MESHACH,
AND ABEDNEGO.

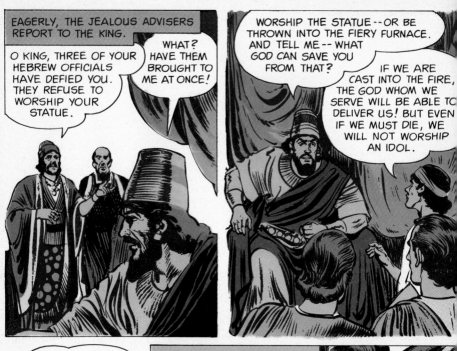

EAGERLY, THE JEALOUS ADVISERS REPORT TO THE KING.

O KING, THREE OF YOUR HEBREW OFFICIALS HAVE DEFIED YOU. THEY REFUSE TO WORSHIP YOUR STATUE.

WHAT? HAVE THEM BROUGHT TO ME AT ONCE!

WORSHIP THE STATUE -- OR BE THROWN INTO THE FIERY FURNACE. AND TELL ME -- WHAT GOD CAN SAVE YOU FROM THAT?

IF WE ARE CAST INTO THE FIRE, THE GOD WHOM WE SERVE WILL BE ABLE TO DELIVER US! BUT EVEN IF WE MUST DIE, WE WILL NOT WORSHIP AN IDOL.

HEAT THE FURNACE -- SEVEN TIMES HOTTER THAN EVER BEFORE -- AND THROW THEM IN IT!

THE THREE HEBREWS ARE QUICKLY BOUND AND THROWN INTO THE RAGING FIRE.

BUT WHEN THE KING LOOKS INTO THE FURNACE...

THEY'RE ALIVE! NOT EVEN TOUCHED BY THE FLAMES! AND, DIDN'T WE CAST **THREE** INTO THE FIRE?

WE DID, O KING.

BUT I SEE **FOUR**! AND THE FOURTH LOOKS LIKE SOMEONE FROM HEAVEN.

SHADRACH! MESHACH! ABEDNEGO! COME OUT!

A King's Boast

FROM DANIEL 3:26—5:6

WHEN KING NEBUCHADNEZZAR SEES THAT DANIEL'S FRIENDS ARE NOT BURNED IN THE FIERY FURNACE, HE IS AFRAID AND ORDERS THEM OUT.

BLESSED BE THE GOD OF SHADRACH, MESHACH AND ABEDNEGO, WHO SENT HIS ANGEL TO SAVE THEM. AND IF ANY MAN DARES TO SAY A WORD AGAINST THEIR GOD, HE WILL DIE!

IT WOULDN'T BE SMART FOR US TO MAKE ANY MORE ATTACKS ON THE HEBREWS.

WHEN THE KING HAS ANOTHER DREAM, HE AGAIN CALLS FOR DANIEL.

NONE OF MY OTHER ADVISERS CAN TELL ME WHAT IT MEANS. CAN YOU?

YES--BUT YOU WILL NOT LIKE IT.

THE KING IS UPSET BY WHAT DANIEL SAYS, BUT IN TIME HE FORGETS... ONE DAY AS HE WALKS IN HIS PALACE ROOF GARDEN...

LOOK AT THE GREAT CITY **I** HAVE BUILT**!** LONG AFTER I AM GONE IT WILL BE A TRIBUTE TO **MY** POWER AND MIGHT**!**

THE TREE YOU DREAMED ABOUT IS YOU, O KING-- TALL, STRONG, AND PROUD. YOU SAW THE TREE CUT DOWN. THIS MEANS THAT YOUR POWER AS KING WILL BE TAKEN FROM YOU IF YOU DO NOT HONOR GOD ABOVE YOURSELF.

AS THE BOASTFUL WORDS ARE SPOKEN, DANIEL'S WARNING COMES TRUE. THE KING LOSES HIS MIND-- AND FOR SEVEN YEARS HE LIVES LIKE A BEAST OF THE FIELD. THEN ONE DAY THE KING REALIZES HE IS BEING PUNISHED FOR FAILING TO HONOR GOD.

O GOD OF DANIEL AND THE HEBREWS, I HONOR AND PRAISE THEE, WHOSE KINGDOM IS GREAT AND EVERLASTING-- WHOSE WORK IS TRUTH AND JUSTICE.

INSTANTLY KING NEBUCHADNEZZAR'S MIND IS RESTORED. HE RETURNS TO THE THRONE AND RULES WISELY WITH DANIEL AS HIS ADVISER.

BUT AFTER HIS DEATH THE RULERS WHO FOLLOW HIM TURN AWAY FROM DANIEL. ONE OF THEM, BELSHAZZAR, IS SO SURE OF HIS OWN WISDOM THAT...

HE LAUGHS AT TWO GREAT THREATS TO HIS KINGDOM: ANGRY PRIESTS WHO ARE TURNING AGAINST HIM, AND THE APPROACH OF THE MIGHTY PERSIAN ARMY. INSTEAD, HE PREPARES A GREAT FEAST TO WHICH HE INVITES A THOUSAND GUESTS...

THE PARTY IS AT ITS MERRIEST WHEN SUDDENLY BELSHAZZAR STARES AT A PLACE HIGH ON THE BANQUET WALL. HE TURNS PALE-- HIS HANDS TREMBLE...

LOOK! ON THE WALL! WHAT IS IT? WHAT DOES IT MEAN?

ndwriting on the Wall

DANIEL 5: 7—6: 14

It is midnight! Outside the walls of Babylon the Persian army waits for traitors within to open the city gates. But inside -- in the banquet hall of the palace -- King Belshazzar eats and drinks merrily with his guests. Suddenly he sees a hand write four words on the wall.

MENE MENE TEKEL UPHARSIN

TERRIFIED, BELSHAZZAR CALLS FOR HIS ADVISERS TO EXPLAIN THE WORDS, BUT THEY CANNOT. WHEN THE KING'S MOTHER HEARS THE EXCITEMENT IN THE BANQUET HALL SHE RUSHES TO HER SON.

MY SON, THERE'S A MAN IN YOUR KINGDOM NAMED DANIEL WHO CAN INTERPRET DREAMS. CALL HIM.

DANIEL! YES! YES! BRING HIM HERE AT ONCE!

NOT A SOUND IS HEARD IN THE GREAT BANQUET HALL UNTIL DANIEL APPEARS BEFORE THE KING.

TELL ME WHAT THOSE WORDS MEAN AND YOU SHALL BE SECOND ONLY TO ME IN ALL BABYLON.

O KING, THEY ARE A WARNING FROM GOD. YOU HAVE BEEN MEASURED AND FOUND LACKING IN THE QUALITIES OF A RULER. YOUR KINGDOM WILL BE GIVEN TO THE PERSIANS.

I DON'T BELIEVE YOUR MESSAGE, BUT I'LL KEEP MY PROMISE. HERE, THIS CHAIN MAKES YOU NEXT TO ME IN ALL THE KINGDOM. NOW, ON WITH THE FEAST!

AS BELSHAZZAR SPEAKS, PERSIAN SOLDIERS SUDDENLY FILL THE HALL--AND TAKE HIM PRISONER.

SOLDIERS? WHERE DID THEY COME FROM? MY GUARDS! WHERE ARE MY GUARDS?

The Lions' Den

ROM DANIEL 6: 16-28

KING DARIUS HAS BEEN TRICKED BY JEALOUS NOBLES INTO SIGNING A LAW THAT CONDEMNS DANIEL TO DEATH.

LOOK! DANIEL DOESN'T SEEM TO BE AFRAID.

HE WILL BE WHEN HE GETS TO THE LIONS' DEN. OUR PLAN TO GET RID OF HIM IS WORKING PERFECTLY.

A FEW MINUTES LATER DANIEL, WHO BROKE THE KING'S LAW BY PRAYING TO GOD, IS CAST INTO THE LIONS' DEN.

MAY THE GOD WHOM YOU SERVE PROTECT YOU.

SEAL THE DEN WITH A STONE SO THAT EVERYONE WILL KNOW I AM ENFORCING THE LAW.

IF ONLY I COULD CHANGE THIS ONE LAW TO SAVE MY FRIEND.

THAT NIGHT THE KING CAN NEITHER EAT NOR SLEEP. HE PACES UP AND DOWN HIS ROOM -- THINKING OF DANIEL.

AT DAYBREAK HE RUSHES TO THE LIONS' DEN.

ROLL AWAY THAT STONE!

DANIEL! DANIEL! DID YOUR GOD PROTECT YOU?

MY GOD HAS SHUT THE LIONS' MOUTHS!

THE KING IS OVERJOYED, AND ORDERS A ROPE THROWN DOWN, AND DANIEL IS PULLED OUT OF THE DEN. THEN HE SENDS FOR THE NOBLES WHO PLOTTED DANIEL'S DEATH.

YOU SENT DANIEL TO THE LIONS -- NOW WE'LL SEE HOW **YOU** LIKE IT!

GUARDS! THROW THEM INTO THE DEN!

THEN DARIUS ISSUES A DECREE...

I, DARIUS, COMMAND ALL PEOPLE IN THIS KINGDOM TO HONOR THE GOD THAT DANIEL WORSHIPS AND SERVES.

AND FOR THE REST OF HIS LIFE, DANIEL HELPS TO RULE BABYLON, THE COUNTRY HE ENTERED AS A CAPTIVE. AGAINST ALL ODDS, HE BOLDLY STANDS FOR GOD-- AND GOD REWARDS HIM.

Twelve Men of God

FROM THE MINOR PROPHETS

THE LAST TWELVE BOOKS OF THE OLD TESTAMENT ARE CALLED THE MINOR PROPHETS. EACH IS NAMED FOR A MAN WHOM GOD CALLED TO SPEAK FOR HIM AT A CRUCIAL TIME IN THE HISTORY OF ISRAEL AND JUDAH.

HOSEA -- the Prophet of Love

HOSEA LOVES HIS WIFE, GOMER, VERY MUCH. BUT ONE DAY SHE RUNS AWAY. HOSEA IS BROKENHEARTED. THEN SUDDENLY HE SEES THAT THE PEOPLE OF ISRAEL HAVE TREATED GOD THE WAY GOMER HAS TREATED HIM. GOD LOVE HIS PEOPLE, BUT THEY HAVE RUN AWAY TO WORSHIP IDOLS.

CAN GOD FORGIVE THEM? "YES," HOSEA SAYS, "FOR I CAN FORGIVE GOMER, AND GOD'S LOVE IS GREATER THAN MINE."

"GOD LOVES YOU. HE WILL FORGIVE YOUR SINS IF YOU CONFESS THEM AND WORSHIP HIM." THIS IS HOSEA'S MESSAGE TO THE PEOPLE OF ISRAEL.

AMOS -- and the Crooked Wall

JOEL -- and the Plague of Locusts

LIKE A MIGHTY ARMY DESTROYING EVERYTHING IN ITS PATH, MILLIONS OF LOCUSTS SWARM OVER THE LAND OF JUDAH. THEY DEVOUR THE CROPS -- LEAVING ONLY BARREN FIELDS BEHIND.

"WHAT WILL WE DO?" THE PEOPLE CRY.

THE PROPHET JOEL ANSWERS: "REPENT OF YOUR SINS. SEEK GOD'S HELP, AND HE WILL RESTORE THE LAND."

THEN HE ADDS THIS PROMISE: "ONE DAY GOD WILL SEND HIS HOLY SPIRIT INTO THE HEARTS OF HIS PEOPLE."

AMOS, A SHEPHERD OF JUDAH, IS WATCHING HIS SHEEP WHEN GOD CALLS HIM TO A DANGEROUS JOB. "GO," GOD SAYS, "TO THE NEIGHBORING COUNTRY OF ISRAEL AND TELL THE PEOPLE THAT THEY ARE GOING TO BE PUNISHED FOR THEIR SINS."

WITHOUT PROTESTING, AMOS ACCEPTS THE JOB AND GOES TO THE CITY OF BETHEL IN ISRAEL.

"PREPARE TO MEET THY GOD," HE TELLS THE PEOPLE OF ISRAEL, "FOR YOU ARE LIKE A CROOKED WALL THAT MUST BE DESTROYED BEFORE A NEW ONE CAN BE BUILT."

OBADIAH --
the Angry Prophet

OBADIAH IS ANGRY AT JUDAH'S NEIGHBOR, THE NATION OF EDOM. "YOU CHEERED," HE CRIES TO EDOM, "WHEN BABYLON DESTROYED JERUSALEM. YOU HELPED TO ROB THE CITY OF ITS TREASURES. YOU CAPTURED THE PEOPLE AS THEY TRIED TO ESCAPE AND TURNED THEM OVER TO THE ENEMY."

THEN HE PREDICTS EDOM'S PUNISHMENT: "BECAUSE YOUR CAPITAL CITY IS PROTECTED BY ROCKY CLIFFS, YOU THINK IT CANNOT BE DESTROYED. BUT IT CAN! AND IT WILL-- AS WILL EVERY NATION THAT DISOBEYS GOD."

JONAH --
the Man Who Ran Away

NINEVEH IS ONE OF THE MOST WICKED CITIES IN THE WORLD. SO, WHEN GOD TELLS JONAH TO GO TO **NINEVEH** WITH A MESSAGE TO SAVE THE CITY FROM ITS ENEMIES, JONAH RUNS THE OTHER WAY.

BUT AFTER A LESSON FROM GOD, JONAH OBEYS. HE TELLS NINEVEH TO REPENT OF ITS SINS -- AND HE PREACHES HIS MESSAGE SO SUCCESSFULLY THAT THE CITY DOES REPENT AND IS SAVED FROM DESTRUCTION.

THE MESSAGE OF THE BOOK OF JONAH IS THIS: GOD LOVES ALL PEOPLE. THOSE WHO KNOW GOD MUST TELL OTHERS ABOUT HIM.

MICAH --
Champion of the Poor

MICAH, A SMALL-TOWN PROPHET, IS A CHAMPION OF THE POOR. HE DARES TO CONDEMN THE WEALTHY LEADERS OF JUDAH AND ISRAEL.

"YOU HATE JUSTICE," HE SHOUTS, "AND YOU OPPRESS THE POOR. BECAUSE YOU DO, JUDAH AND ISRAEL HAVE BECOME SO WEAK AND CORRUPT THAT THEY WILL BE DESTROYED."

WHEN THE PEOPLE ASK WHAT GOD EXPECTS THEM TO DO, MICAH ANSWERS: "DO JUSTLY, LOVE MERCY, AND WALK HUMBLY WITH THY GOD."

AND TO THOSE WHO WILL LISTEN HE MAKES A WONDERFUL PROMISE: "IN THE LITTLE TOWN OF BETHLEHEM A SAVIOR WILL BE BORN--A SAVIOR WHOSE KINGDOM OF PEACE WILL LAST FOREVER."

NAHUM
Condemns a City

WHEN THE PROPHET JONAH WARNED **NINEVEH** OF ITS WICKEDNESS, THE CITY REPENTED-- AND WAS SPARED.

NOW, ONE HUNDRED AND FIFTY YEARS LATER, ANOTHER PROPHET, NAHUM, IS CALLED TO CONDEMN **NINEVEH** FOR RETURNING TO A LIFE OF SIN.

"THE LORD IS SLOW TO ANGER," NAHUM TELLS THE CITY, "BUT HE IS NOT BLIND. HE WILL NOT LET THE WICKED GO UNPUNISHED."

THIS TIME THE CITY IS NOT SPARED-- THE ARMIES OF BABYLON SO COMPLETELY DESTROY **NINEVEH** THAT IT IS NEVER REBUILT.

HABAKKUK--
The Man Who Asks Questions

HABAKKUK IS A MAN WHO ASKS QUESTIONS-- OF GOD.

HABAKKUK: THE PEOPLE OF JUDAH ARE GETTING MORE WICKED EVERY DAY. HOW LONG WILL THEY GO UNPUNISHED?

GOD: NOT FOR LONG. THE BABYLONIANS ARE COMING. I AM USING THEM TO TEACH JUDAH THAT EVIL MUST BE DESTROYED.

HABAKKUK: THE BABYLONIANS? AREN'T THEY MORE WICKED THAN JUDAH?

GOD: YES, BUT HAVE FAITH. IN TIME YOU WILL UNDERSTAND MY PLANS.

IN THE MIDST OF ALL THE EVIL AROUND HIM, HABAKKUK IS COMFORTED IN KNOWING THAT GOD IS IN CHARGE OF THE WORLD. "GOD IS IN HIS HOLY TEMPLE," HABAKKUK SAYS, "AND NO MATTER WHAT HAPPENS, I AM NOT AFRAID, FOR THE LORD IS MY STRENGTH."

ZECHARIAH and the Triumphal Entry

ZECHARIAH IS A FRIEND OF HAGGAI AND WORKS WITH HIM TO REBUILD THE TEMPLE IN JERUSALEM.

ZEPHANIAH: Repent or Die

"THE DAY OF THE LORD IS AT HAND," ZEPHANIAH WARNED JUDAH. "GOD WILL PUNISH ALL NATIONS OF THE EARTH THAT HAVE DISOBEYED HIM. NEITHER GOLD NOR SILVER WILL BE ABLE TO DELIVER THOSE WHO HAVE TURNED FROM GOD."

ZEPHANIAH PLEADS WITH HIS PEOPLE TO REPENT AND SEEK GOD'S FORGIVENESS. "THOSE WHO DO," HE PROMISES, "WILL LIVE IN PEACE UNDER THE RULE OF GOD."

HAGGAI -- A Temple Builder

WHEN THE HEBREWS FIRST RETURN TO JERUSALEM--AFTER YEARS OF CAPTIVITY IN BABYLON--THEIR FIRST THOUGHT IS TO REBUILD THE TEMPLE. THEY START-- BUT THEY SOON GET DISCOURAGED AND QUIT. FOR FIFTEEN YEARS NOTHING IS DONE.

GOD SPEAKS TO HAGGAI AND HE TAKES THE MESSAGE TO THE PEOPLE.

"BUILD GOD'S TEMPLE," HE PREACHES. AND IN FOUR YEARS IT IS BUILT!

MALACHI -- The Final Warning

THE PEOPLE OF JUDAH HAVE RETURNED TO JERUSALEM FROM CAPTIVITY IN BABYLON-- THE TEMPLE HAS BEEN REBUILT. BUT STILL THEY ARE UNHAPPY. AND MALACHI TELLS THEM WHY--

"YOU DO NOT SHOW RESPECT TO GOD. YOU WOULD NOT DARE BRING CHEAP GIFTS TO THE GOVERNOR. YET YOU BRING CHEAP AND FAULTY OFFERINGS TO GOD."

"GOD KNOWS THOSE WHO ARE FAITHFUL TO HIM. HE WILL REWARD THEM. BUT THE UNFAITHFUL WILL PERISH AS STUBBLE IN THE BURNING FIELDS AFTER THE HARVEST."

The Final Message

THE VOICE OF THE PROPHET MALACHI IS THE LAST TO BE HEARD IN THE STORY OF THE OLD TESTAMENT. BUT BEFORE WE HEAR HIS FINAL MESSAGE--WHICH IS FOUND IN THE BOOK THAT BEARS HIS NAME -- LET US BRIEFLY REVIEW THE HISTORY OF THE PEOPLE TO WHOM HE SPOKE.

IN OUR STORY OF THE BIBLE WE HAVE BEEN TRACING THE LIVES OF THE PEOPLE WHO DESCENDED FROM ABRAHAM. GOD CALLED HIM TO BE THE FATHER OF A NATION THAT WOULD TEACH THE WORLD ABOUT THE ONE TRUE GOD. ABRAHAM OBEYED GOD AND WENT TO CANAAN WHERE HIS FAMILY LIVED AND GREW. HIS GRANDSON, JACOB (OR ISRAEL), BECAME THE FATHER OF 12 SONS. THEIR FAMILIES WERE CALLED THE 12 TRIBES OF ISRAEL.

WHEN A FAMINE STRUCK CANAAN THE TRIBES WENT DOWN TO EGYPT WHERE THEY LIVED FOR MANY YEARS. BUT AFTER A TIME THE EGYPTIANS TURNED AGAINST THE ISRAELITES AND FORCED THEM TO WORK AS SLAVES. THE PEOPLE CRIED TO GOD FOR HELP...

GOD HEARD THE CRIES OF HIS PEOPLE AND SENT MOSES TO LEAD THEM OUT OF EGYPT -- ACROSS THE RED SEA -- AND BACK TO THE PROMISED LAND OF CANAAN. WITH GOD'S HELP THEY CONQUERED THE LAND AND MADE IT THEIR HOME. FOR MANY YEARS JUDGES RULED OVER THE TRIBES OF ISRAEL, BUT THE PEOPLE LONGED FOR A KING.

GOD HEARD THEIR PLEA AND GAVE THEM A KING, SAUL. HE WAS FOLLOWED BY DAVID, WHO BUILT ISRAEL INTO A POWERFUL NATION. BUT IN THE YEARS THAT FOLLOWED, THE PEOPLE TURNED FROM GOD TO WORSHIP IDOLS. THEY QUARRELED AMONG THEMSELVES, AND THE NATION WAS SPLIT INTO TWO KINGDOMS -- ISRAEL IN THE NORTH AND JUDAH IN THE SOUTH. WEAK AND CORRUPT, THEY WERE OPEN TO THE ATTACKS OF STRONGER NATIONS AROUND THEM.

IN TIME BOTH KINGDOMS WERE CONQUERED. MANY OF THE PEOPLE WERE TAKEN AWAY TO FOREIGN LANDS. AFTER 70 YEARS OF CAPTIVITY, THE JEWS WERE ALLOWED TO RETURN TO JUDAH AND REBUILD JERUSALEM.

BUT STILL THE PEOPLE WERE UNHAPPY, AND THE PROPHET MALACHI TELLS THEM WHY...

DO YOU CALL THAT GOD'S SHARE OF YOUR GRAIN? HOW CAN YOU BE HAPPY WHEN YOU ROB GOD? BRING YOUR RIGHTFUL GIFTS AND OFFERINGS TO GOD, AND YOU WILL PROSPER.

BUT PEOPLE WHO CHEAT AND BRING NONE OF THEIR GRAIN TO THE TEMPLE PROSPER MORE THAN WE DO.

GOD KNOWS WHO LOVES AND OBEYS HIM. HE WILL REWARD THE RIGHTEOUS AND PUNISH THE WICKED.

WHEN WILL HE DO THIS?

FIRST, GOD WILL SEND A PROPHET AS HIS MESSENGER TO GET THE PEOPLE READY. THEN THE LORD HIMSELF WILL COME AND DELIVER HIS OWN PEOPLE FROM EVIL. BUT HE WILL DESTROY THE WICKED WHO DISOBEY.

SO, WITH A WARNING -- AND A PROMISE -- THE OLD TESTAMENT ENDS. BUT TO THE JEWS THE QUESTION REMAINS: WHEN WILL THE GREAT DELIVERER COME?